Five Easy Steps to a
Balanced Math Program
for Primary Grades

What Educators and Leaders Are Saying about *Five Easy Steps*

We are using this framework extensively in our school district. Five Easy Steps to a Balanced Math Program *helps teachers focus on teaching concepts for understanding, as opposed to marching through a textbook. We emphasize that our state standards are our curriculum, and this is the framework we are using to plan and teach these standards for understanding to our students. Textbooks, like any other resource, are incidental to the implementation of quality math teaching and learning. We are working toward conceptual understanding and not just teaching the procedures of math the same way we were all taught math. Our teachers are excited about Math Review and Mental Math. Our students are excited about the Problem of the Week. We are all excited about math in our district and the results we are getting with our students.*

> Virginia P. Foley, Ed.D.
> Director of Elementary Curriculum
> and Student Services
> Dalton Public Schools
> Dalton, GA

Five Easy Steps *has strengthened our traditional math curriculum by providing our elementary staff with solid foundation in research-based math instruction. The implementation process focused on the consistency of strategies across the grades and gave the teachers a common language for discussing Mental Math, Math Review, concept development, and problem solving. After three years of implementation, our district continues to show impressive gains on the state assessments for all the NCLB subgroups.*

> Susan Schwicardi, Ed.D.
> Assistant Superintendent for
> Curriculum and Instruction
> District 45
> Villa Park, IL

Five Easy Steps to a Balanced Math Program *provides our teachers with a framework for culturally responsive teaching in mathematics. The framework not only has the flexibility necessary to customize math instruction for students at varying instructional levels, it also encourages collaboration among teachers as they design problem-solving tasks and assessments. The framework and its consistent facilitation in our classrooms have raised the bar for student learning and expectations in mathematics.*

Sharon I. Smith
Principal, Harrison Hill
Elementary School
Metropolitan School District
of Lawrence Township
Indianapolis, IN

The processes outlined in Five Easy Steps *became a critical component of our district's Mathematics Strategic Plan beginning in 1998.* Five Easy Steps to a Balanced Math Program *provided practical suggestions to assist our teachers with the implementation of the district's mathematics program, [including] its required instructional components. While the Mathematics Strategic Plan serves as an umbrella for the district's efforts,* Five Easy Steps to a Balanced Math Program *provided clarity of purpose and a systemic way of maintaining the focus.*

As a result, student achievement has steadily increased while the achievement gap has narrowed. Our work with Five Easy Steps to a Balanced Math Program *has been one of the factors responsible for these improved results.*

Denise M. Walston
Senior Coordinator—Mathematics(K–12)
Norfolk Public Schools
Norfolk, VA

I love the Five Easy Steps *concept because it gives elementary classroom teachers a way to organize and differentiate the daily mathematics instruction. As a principal, I especially love it because I don't have to buy any special text, series, program, or curriculum. This approach fits right into any current program. My teachers love the* Five Easy Steps *mostly because it was developed by two "real" teachers. Larry Ainsworth and Jan Christinson are not just talking theory; they've been there!!!!*

Paula Shaw-Powell
Principal, Double Churches
Elementary School
Muscogee County School District
Columbus, GA

Our use of the Five Easy Steps to a Balanced Math Program *framework has made an astounding difference in our students' ability to reason, think, and be successful in math! The framework provides for a variety of learning experiences that have helped our teachers learn how to differentiate mathematics learning for our students and help them to develop conceptual understanding of math topics. The student success is apparent in their daily classroom activities and is being transferred to our statewide testing results. We love it!*

Jodi Peyton
Digital Age Literacy Coach
Metropolitan School District
of Lawrence Township
Indianapolis, IN

Five Easy Steps to a Balanced Math Program *has transformed math instruction at Sunnyside Elementary! The framework has provided a balanced plan for instruction; it ensures that nothing important gets left out! Best of all, our student achievement on standardized tests has dramatically improved!*

Connie Thomas, Ed.S.
Principal, Sunnyside Elementary
Metropolitan School District
of Lawrence Township
Indianapolis, IN

Using the Five Easy Steps to a Balanced Math Program *has brought consistency to understanding and developing math concepts for our* teachers *and* students. *Teachers are collaborating on developing mathematical experiences for students, which has allowed the students to construct a deep conceptual understanding of mathematical strategies and skills.* The Five Easy Steps to a Balanced Math Program *has been our key to designing best-practice instruction for student growth.*

> Cathy Hargrove
> Digital Age Literacy Coach
> Harrison Hill Elementary
> Metropolitan School District
> of Lawrence Township
> Indianapolis, IN

Five Easy Steps to a Balanced Math Program *is a book that provides simple-to-follow strategies for improving student learning in math. The ideas presented are easy to adapt to a teacher's personal style without investing enormous sums of money and effort in another passing trend.*

> Brenda Wolfe, Ed.D.
> Principal, Crestview Elementary
> Metropolitan School District
> of Lawrence Township
> Indianapolis, IN

The format of Five Easy Steps to a Balanced Math Program *provided the skeleton that our teachers needed and used to structure their math lessons. The "steps" were easy to follow and they facilitated the implementation of our state standards. Teachers were able to work as teams to compile daily Math Review reinforcement lessons, problems of the week to reiterate a concept, and Mental Math problems to engage and motivate students.*

> Estella Haynes Swann
> Math Facilitator
> Crestview Elementary School
> Metropolitan School District
> of Lawrence Township
> Indianapolis, IN

Five Easy Steps to a Balanced Math Program has revolutionized the way our teachers approach math instruction! The five steps not only represent best practice, they are easy to understand and can be implemented by our teachers immediately following awareness/training sessions. The philosophy of the five steps reinforces our desire to create mathematically powerful students. *Five Easy Steps to a Balanced Math Program* is so highly regarded in our school district, it has made our list of "non-negotiable" professional practices!

Michele Walker
Mathematics/Science/Assessment
Coordinator
Metropolitan School District
of Wayne Township
Indianapolis, IN

Five Easy Steps to a Balanced Math Program for Primary Grades

Larry Ainsworth

Jan Christinson

ISBN: 9798750717125

Contents

Acknowledgments   xv

About the Authors   xix

Introduction   xxiii
The Need for a Balanced Math Program   xxiii
Designing the Balanced Math Program   xxviii
Organization of This Book   xxx
As We Begin   xxxi

PART ONE   THE FIVE EASY STEPS   1

Chapter 1   Step 1: Computational Skills
                        (Math Review and Mental Math)   3
Essential Questions   3
Rationale   3
Description of Step 1: Math Review Component   4
    A Deliberate Selection of Problems   5
    The Math Review Template   6
    Math Review Progression through Primary Grade Span   7
    The Teacher's Role During Math Review   8
    Processing Math Review   9
    Other Important Ways to Process Math Review   10
Assessment: The Math Review Quiz   14
Essential Questions   14
Rationale   14
    The Math Review Quiz   15
    A Sample Math Review Quiz   17
    Scoring the Math Review Quiz   17
    Math Review Quiz Self-Reflection   18
    Tutors and Tutees   19
    The Home Connection and Extra Practice   20
    Benefits of the Math Review Quiz   21

Contents

Differentiation   22

Description of Step 1: Mental Math Component   24

Essential Questions   24

Rationale   24

    How to Implement Mental Math   25

    Mental Math Benefits   28

Reader's Assignment   28

Chapter 2   Step 2: Problem Solving   **31**

Essential Questions   31

Rationale   31

Description of Step 2   33

    Selecting the Problem-Solving Task   33

    Teaching Students to Solve the Problem-Solving Task   35

    Problem-Solving Strategies   40

    Problem-Solving Steps for Primary Students   41

    An Investment of Time   45

    Suggested Problem-Solving Sequence for Grades K–2   45

Differentiation   46

Formally Assessing Problem Solving   47

    Creating a Problem-Solving Rubric   48

    How to Design the Problem-Solving Rubric   50

    Using the Rubric to Assess   53

    Benefits of the Problem-Solving and
Rubric Assessment Process   56

Reader's Assignment   57

Chapter 3   Step 3: Conceptual Understanding   **59**

Essential Questions   59

Definitions   59

Rationale   60

Contents

The Conceptual Understanding Unit of Study   61

Designing a Conceptual Unit   62

     The Value of Planning a Unit Collaboratively   64

Primary Example of Conceptual Unit Planning   76

Other Considerations   78

The Knowledge Package Process   78

Differentiation and Vocabulary Development   81

Reader's Assignment   84

Chapter 4   Step 4: Mastery of Math Facts   **85**

Essential Questions   85

Rationale   85

Implementing Step 4   86

     Emphasize Patterns   86

     Determine Grade-Appropriate Facts   87

     Inform Parents at Beginning of Year   89

     Establish Timeline to Assess Progress   89

     Assess What Students Presently Know   90

     Provide Daily Practice Materials   90

     Math Review and Mental Math   92

A Simple Management System   92

Helping Students Handle Time Pressure   93

     When It Is Time to Start Assessing   94

     Assessment Day   95

     Extra Practice Required   96

Differentiation: Strategies for Struggling Students   96

Summing Up   97

Reader's Assignment   98

Chapter 5   Step 5: Common Formative Assessment   **99**

Essential Questions   99

Contents

Overview   99

Rationale   100

Power Standards   101

Vertical Alignment   103

Beginning with the End in Mind   106

Designing the Common Formative Assessment   106

    The Implementation Sequence   107

The Big Picture—How All the Practices Connect   109

Implementation   112

Benefits   113

Reader's Assignment   114

PART TWO   INSIDE THE PRIMARY CLASSROOM   **115**

Chapter 6   **Inside the Kindergarten Classroom**   **117**

Step 1   Kindergarten Computational Skills (Math Review and Mental Math)   117

    The Math Review Template   117

    The Math Review Quiz   119

    Mental Math   119

Step 2   Kindergarten Problem Solving   120

    The Problem-Solving Teaching Sequence to Follow Throughout the Year   120

    Sample Kindergarten Problem-Solving Task   121

    Transition During the School Year   122

Step 3   Kindergarten Conceptual Understanding   122

Step 4   Kindergarten Mastery of Math Facts   125

Step 5   Common Formative Assessment   126

Contents

Chapter 7   Inside the Grade 1 Classroom   127

**Step 1   First-Grade Computational Skills
(Math Review and Mental Math)   127**

The Math Review Template   127

The Math Review Quiz   130

Mental Math   131

Step 2   First-Grade Problem Solving   132

The Problem-Solving Teaching Sequence
for the Beginning of the Year   132

The Problem-Solving Teaching Sequence
for the Middle of the School Year   133

The Problem-Solving Teaching Sequence
for the End of the School Year   133

Sample Grade 1 Problem-Solving Task   134

Step 3   First-Grade Conceptual Understanding   135

Step 4   First-Grade Mastery of Math Facts   139

Step 5   Common Formative Assessment   140

Chapter 8   Inside the Grade 2 Classroom   141

**Step 1   Second-Grade Computational Skills
(Math Review and Mental Math)   141**

The Math Review Template   141

The Math Review Quiz   144

Mental Math   145

Step 2   Second-Grade Problem Solving   146

The Problem-Solving Teaching Sequence for
the Beginning and Middle of the School Year   146

The Problem-Solving Teaching Sequence
for the End of the School Year   146

Sample Grade 2 Problem-Solving Task   146

Step 3   Second-Grade Conceptual Understanding   148

Contents

Step 4 Second-Grade Mastery of Math Facts   151

Step 5 Common Formative Assessment   152

PART THREE RESOURCES FOR IMPLEMENTATION   **155**

Chapter 9   Putting It All Together: Time Management
              and Frequently Asked Questions   **157**

Part 1 Time Management   157

        A Second-Grade Math Schedule   158

Part 2 Frequently Asked Questions   162

        Step 1: Computational Skills
               (Math Review and Mental Math)   162

        Step 2: Problem Solving   170

        Step 3: Conceptual Understanding   174

        Step 4: Mastery of Math Facts   180

Closing Thoughts   183

Chapter 10   Guidelines for School Leaders   **185**

Executive Summary   185

Math Leadership Team Planning Questions   190

Alignment Diagram   194

A Framework for Implementation   196

Reproducibles   **207**

References and Other Resources   **243**

        References   243

        Webliography of Online Math   245

        Suggested Reading   250

Index   **251**

Acknowledgments

Since the initial publication of *Five Easy Steps to a Balanced Math Program* in 2000, math educators and leaders nationwide have found the framework of these five steps to be effective for designing and delivering the key components of a comprehensive math program. It was this success that led to our decision to write three separate books—one each for the primary, upper elementary, and secondary grades—rather than one second edition attempting to address kindergarten through high school grades. We wish to acknowledge and thank our former publisher, Anne Fenske of Advanced Learning Press (now Lead Learn Press), for her diligent support of and commitment to this project. We also wish to extend our special thanks to George Foster of Foster Covers, Brooke Graves of Graves Editorial Service, and Karen Hammon of Graphic Advantage, who have worked diligently to prepare these books for publication.

We would also like to deeply acknowledge the work of Marilyn Burns, Liping Ma, John Van De Walle, the National Council of Teachers of Mathematics, and the Trends In Math and Science Studies (TIMSS) researchers James Hiebert and Jim Stigler. Their individual and collective work have played a key role in developing the concepts and procedures upon which this framework is based.

Special thanks to all the leaders and educators across the United States who have attended the *Five Easy Steps to a Balanced Math Program* workshops and applied the steps in their own schools and districts. In particular, we want to recognize and thank five urban school districts that have made the *Five Easy Steps* framework their district-wide mathematics initiative of choice: Norfolk Public Schools in Norfolk, Virginia; the Metropolitan School District of Wayne Township in Indianapolis, Indiana; the Muscogee County School District of Columbus, Georgia; Villa Park District #45 in Villa Park, Illinois; and Dalton Public Schools in Dalton, Georgia.

Acknowledgments

Owing to the leadership and vision of Dr. Denise Walston, Norfolk Public Schools became the first major school district in the nation to adopt the Five Easy Steps model. Dr. Terry Thompson, Dr. Karen Gould, Michele Walker, and Dr. Lisa Lantrip of Wayne Township have continued to advocate and refine *Five Easy Steps* as their district math initiative for all elementary and junior high schools. Principal Judy Stegemann and other elementary principals in Wayne Township continue to support their teachers in the full implementation of the program. Dr. Karen Greyor, Dr. Shelia Barefield, Dr. Maxine Lee, and Dr. Paula Shaw-Powell of Muscogee County Schools selected *Five Easy Steps* as the district's math framework for K–7 schools beginning with the 2005–06 school year. Dr. Susan Schwicardi of Villa Park District #45, near Chicago, first saw the potential for improving student achievement in math through the *Five Easy Steps* program several years ago and made it a district initiative at that time. Dr. Virginia Foley, Executive Director of Student Services in the school district of Dalton Public Schools, Dalton, Georgia, continues to advocate the implementation of the *Five Easy Steps* framework within her district's schools. We are sincerely grateful to these leaders and their educators for their diligence and commitment to this program that is improving student achievement in mathematics.

We also wish to thank and commend the Metropolitan School District of Lawrence Township in Indianapolis, Indiana. Under the leadership of Dr. Marcia Capuano, Dr. Jan Combs, and Dr. Walter Bourke, several of their elementary and all of their middle schools have implemented the *Five Easy Steps* model. Two schools in particular, Crestview Elementary and Harrison Hill Elementary, embarked upon a multiyear partnership with The Leadership and Learning Center (formerly the Center for Performance Assessment)

Acknowledgments

to fully implement, in every grade level, each of the *Five Easy Steps*. Under the leadership of Crestview's principal, Dr. Brenda Wolfe, and her math and literacy coaches, Dr. Judith Larr and Dr. Estella Swann, Crestview students made dramatic gains in their mathematics scores on the Indiana state assessment. Under the leadership of Harrison Hill's principal, Dr. Sharon Smith, and her math and literacy coaches, Cathy Hargrove and Jodi Peyton, Harrison Hill students have also shown major improvement in mathematics performance. More recently, the faculties of Sunnyside Elementary and Oaklandon Elementary, under the leadership of principals Connie Thomas and Doris Downing, respectively, have committed to full implementation of the *Five Easy Steps* framework. Special thanks to math and literacy coach Kimberly Brown for her assistance and support.

We would like to extend special thanks to the many math educators from across the country who gave us permission to publish their math performance assessment examples in Step 3.

About the Authors

Larry Ainsworth was the Executive Director of Professional Development at the Leadership and Learning Center in Englewood, Colorado, from 1999-2013. Currently an independent author-consultant, Larry has presented professional learning workshops and keynotes in school systems throughout the U.S., and in Canada, Argentina, and Switzerland.

Larry's published books include: *Rigorous Curriculum Design, 2nd Edition* (2019), *Common Formative Assessments 2.0* (2015), *"Unwrapping" the Common Core* (2014), *Prioritizing the Common Core* (2013), *Rigorous Curriculum Design* (2010), *Common Formative Assessments* (2006), *"Unwrapping" the Standards* (2003), *Power Standards* (2003), *Five Easy Steps to a Balanced Math Program* (2000 and 2006), and *Student Generated Rubrics* (1998). A popular workshop Larry created, "Teacher Clarity: Learning Intentions and Success Criteria" (2016), is a step-by-step process that PK-12 educators use to bring clarity to student learning targets.

Throughout his career as an education consultant, Larry has worked on site in school systems to assist leaders and educators in understanding and implementing "timeless" practices: prioritizing and "unwrapping" state standards, developing common formative assessments, designing authentic performance tasks, and creating rigorous curricular units of study in all content areas, pre-kindergarten through grade 12— all to increase teacher efficacy.

Larry has delivered keynote addresses nationwide, most notably for the U.S. Department of Education, New York Department of Education, Ohio Department of Education, Michigan Department of Education, Connecticut Department of Education, Connecticut Technical High School System, Colorado Department of Education,

Harvard University Graduate School of Education's Principals' Center, Indiana ASCD, Indiana Computer Educators' Conference, California ASCD, California Private Schools' Association, Ohio's Battelle for Kids Conference, University of Southern Maine, Virginia Title I and STARS conferences, and the Southern Regional Education Board. He conducted breakout sessions at national and regional conferences throughout the country, most notably for the California Math Council, the California International Studies Project, the Alabama CLAS Summer Institute, the Delaware Professional Development Conference, the National Council of Teachers of Mathematics, the National Association for Supervision and Curriculum Development, and the National School Conference Institute.

With 24 years' experience as an upper elementary and middle school classroom teacher in demographically diverse schools, Larry brings a varied background and wide range of professional experiences to each of his presentations. He has held numerous leadership roles within school districts, including mentor teacher and K–12 math committee co-chair, and has served as a mathematics assessment consultant in several San Diego County school districts.

Larry holds a Master of Science degree in educational administration.

For questions or feedback regarding the implementation of *Five Easy Steps to a Balanced Math Program,* please contact the author at:

Larry Ainsworth
larry@larryainsworth.com
www.larryainsworth.com

About the Authors

Jan Christinson has been a Distinguished Teacher-in-Residence in the College of Education at California State University at San Marcos and was a consultant for The Leadership and Learning Center (formerly the Center for Performance Assessment) located in Englewood, Colorado. With 30 years of teaching experience at the elementary, middle school, and university levels, Jan consulted with school districts and teachers across the country to help improve classroom instruction in mathematics. In addition to the three editions of *Five Easy Steps to a Balanced Math Program* (2006), Jan has co-authored *Student-Generated Rubrics, Five Easy Steps to a Balanced Math Program* (with Larry Ainsworth), and *Writing Prompts for Middle School Mathematics*. His 2013 book, *Balancing Mathematics Instruction*, presents highly effective and practical ways to implement the Common Core math standards.

Throughout his teaching career, Jan held various leadership positions, including mentor teacher, math department chair, K–12 math committee co-chair, and summer school principal. He presented assessment workshops for beginning teacher support groups in California and helped teacher candidates prepare for basic skills tests that have been part of the teacher credentialing process. He presented dynamic, "how to" sessions at regional math conferences, and participated in assessment projects for the San Diego County Office of Education.

Jan holds a Master's degree in education.

For questions or feedback regarding the implementation of *Five Easy Steps to a Balanced Math Program,* contact the author at:

Jan Christinson
janchristinson@gmail.com

Introduction

The Need for a Balanced Math Program

How can teachers produce mathematically powerful students—students who can solve problems and also communicate their understanding to others? Our extensive experience as elementary and middle school math teachers has proven that when students are engaged in a "balance" of mathematics activities, they *can* succeed where it counts: in applying their math skills and reasoning ability to solve real-life problems requiring mathematical solutions. By *balance* we mean the deliberate design of instruction and assessment that helps students:

Build computational skills

Develop mathematical reasoning and problem-solving abilities

Deepen conceptual understanding

Demonstrate understanding in a variety of assessment formats

Since the first edition of *Five Easy Steps to a Balanced Math Program: A Practical Guide for K-8 Classroom Teachers* was published in 2000, we have received an increasingly enthusiastic reception to this framework in schools and districts we have worked with across the nation. These five steps are practical, they make sense, and they are easy to understand and implement. They are designed according to recommendations for effective mathematics instruction and assessment from some of the most highly regarded authorities working in mathematics education today.

Busy teachers typically begin implementing these steps in the order in which they are presented in the book. Once the teachers have their Math Review and Mental Math practices (step 1) in place, they introduce the problem-solving process (step 2), followed by the design of a conceptual unit focused on a particular math topic essential for student understanding (step 3). Because student mastery of math facts (step 4) is as important to success in mathematical procedures and reasoning as learning the alphabet is to reading and writing, elementary school faculties distribute or "map" the teaching of these facts across the grades, consciously planning so that students can master the facts before they enter middle school.

Periodically, grade-level teachers at the elementary level and course-specific teachers at the secondary level want to know how students are doing relative to a particular set of math standards that they are all teaching to their students. Hence, they design, administer, score, and analyze a common formative math assessment (step 5) at various intervals throughout the year to assess for learning, so that they can adjust and differentiate instruction to meet the diverse learning needs of their students. With the *Five Easy Steps* framework in mind, teachers implement, one by one, each of these five interconnected steps to produce mathematically powerful students!

We believe teachers are feeling the frustration of the times, wanting to provide their students with a strong math program but not really feeling confident in their ability to do so. Three challenges must be addressed:

1. *Many teachers have not received sufficient professional development in mathematics.*

    The result can be resistance to math programs that emphasize conceptual understanding over computational mastery. Without ongoing professional development in current methodology,

Introduction

educators often resort to teaching math by the familiar, procedure-driven way they learned when they themselves were students.

Achieving different results requires a different approach. Teachers need a new way to organize their math programs—a simple framework for teaching all the essential mathematical components—and the continuing support to confidently implement that framework.

2. *Many teachers feel that their district math programs are confusing, have too many components to include in a math lesson, and address too many standards to cover in the course of one school year.*

The result for these teachers can be the uncomfortable feeling that they are not doing enough, that there are too many learning objectives to work into each day's lesson, and that there is not enough time to do it all. The problem is compounded if these teachers have not received sufficient professional development to experience a paradigm shift in the way they view mathematics education, a shift that helps them:

- Encourage students to look for multiple ways to tackle a new problem
- Value students' understanding and the ability to communicate that understanding verbally and in writing
- Promote problem-solving skills and conceptual understanding over memorization of computational procedures and formulas.

In addition, many teachers perceive gaps or holes in their district-adopted math programs, and recognize the need to

> *Teachers need a new way to organize their math programs—a simple framework for teaching all the essential mathematical components—and the support to confidently implement that framework.*

supplement the district programs with lessons and math activities from other sources. This further increases their anxiety over being able to accomplish everything students need for mathematical success.

To address this challenge, we suggest:

- An organizational structure for providing students with the necessary components of a balanced math program, regardless of the math series in use
- A framework for planning instruction that aligns instruction, learning activities, and assessments around a particular math focus

Working from a viewpoint based on balance, teachers can more effectively pace their instructional activities throughout the school year. They can confidently make their own instructional decisions rather than letting the teacher's edition of the textbook drive instruction. They can more effectively utilize the math textbook and select supplementary materials for specific instructional purposes when appropriate. In short, they can better meet the learning needs of *all* their students.

3. *Many teachers feel pressured to make sure that their students achieve satisfactory scores on high-stakes achievement tests, often at the expense of teaching math in ways they know will develop their students' conceptual understanding and problem-solving abilities.*

Too often, what results is a binary choice: *either* emphasize computational skills and memorization of formulas all year long, to prepare students to do well on the state tests; *or* deemphasize those tested skills so as to teach in-depth lessons designed to promote conceptual understanding. Teachers who choose the latter approach often resolve their accountability anxiety by reluctantly putting aside their conceptual math lessons for the month prior to the test, and substituting drill-and-kill instruction on what students are likely to be tested on.

We think the solution lies not in a binary choice of computation *or* conceptual understanding, but rather a blend of computation *and* conceptual understanding. Such a solution may seem intellectually obvious, yet for many teachers the question remains, "*How* do I effectively combine both?" Here is how we answered that question for ourselves.

We focus on math computation practice during the first part of *every* math lesson, to help students sharpen and maintain their math skills *over time.* This consistent, daily practice results in students retaining those skills, as opposed to the short-term (and short-lived) recall that comes from cramming for a test.

We then devote the remainder of the math lesson to conceptual understanding and problem solving. In this way, we prepare our students for the full range of multiple assessment measures they will eventually encounter, from the all-important state assessment to district and classroom assessments, while simultaneously providing them with the skills and understanding needed to successfully solve math-related problems throughout their lives.

Developing a balanced math program is the answer for teachers who want to ensure that their students are receiving the full range of mathematical understanding and skills. The purpose of this book is to share with other teachers the methods we have successfully developed for doing just this. We take readers

> *Developing a balanced math program is the answer for teachers who want to ensure that their students are receiving the full range of mathematical understanding and skills.*

step-by-step through each of the five steps in our balanced math program model, describing in an easy-to-follow sequence how to implement the program successfully in primary-grade classrooms.

Designing the Balanced Math Program

Five Easy Steps to a Balanced Math Program: A Practical Guide for K-8 Classroom Teachers (2000) introduced five essential components for developing an effective mathematics program. Based on the National Council of Teachers of Mathematics (NCTM) recommendations, the book provided math educators in elementary and middle schools with a practical framework for implementing each of these components.

As a result of presenting the *Five Easy Steps* seminar and assisting teachers in the implementation of these ideas over the past six years, we realized the need to update this information. We wanted to make it more specific to particular grade spans (K–2, 3–5, and (6–8) and to the individual grades within each of those grade spans.In addition, the framework proved equally relevant and useful for the first two years of high school. For these reasons, we decided to publish three books—one each for the primary, upper elementary,and secondary grades—rather than one K–10 book as an expandedsecond edition. These three books are titled: *Five Easy Steps to a Balanced Math Program for **Primary** Grades; Five Easy Steps to a Balanced Math Program for **Upper Elementary** Grades;* and *FiveEasy Steps to a Balanced Math Program for Secondary Grades.*

Readers familiar with the original book will find that these new publications enhance their understanding of the five steps and show how to implement the steps more effectively within their classrooms and schools.

Introduction

The five main components of the *Five Easy Steps to a Balanced MathProgram* are summarized here.

Step 1: Computational Skills (Math Review and Mental Math). Math Review emphasizes the development of number sense as students practice procedural mathematics and computational skillsevery day. It also prepares students for success on the annual state mathematics assessment. **Mental Math** helps students become skillful in computing math problems mentally.

Step 2: Problem Solving. This step provides both a structure for problem-solving activities related to the current conceptual unitfocus and a general problem-solving rubric or scoring guide that is used throughout the year to assess student work.

Step 3: Conceptual Understanding. Step 3 begins by identifying, in district and state math standards, a particular grade-level topic that is essential for student understanding. That topic becomes the focus of a conceptual math unit that is deliberately designed to align instruction with an end-of-unit assessment.

Step 4: Mastery of Math Facts. The emphasis in step 4 is on factrecall through student understanding of patterns. A program of accountability enables students to learn all their basic math facts by the end of elementary school. The process begins with the faculty mapping all of the addition, subtraction, multiplication, anddivision facts across grades K–5.

Step 5: Common Formative Assessment. The final step aligns school-based assessments *for* learning to math Power Standards. These formative assessments are collaboratively designed, administered, scored, and analyzed within each grade level several times throughout the school year. Common formative assessments provide teachers with valid feedback as to students' current understanding of the Power Standards in focus. Such data provide predictive value regarding how students are likely to perform on subsequent district and state assessments—in time for teachers to modify and adjust instruction to meet specific learning needs.

Organization of This Book

The book has been organized into three major parts. **Part One** describes each of the five steps and the application of each step to the primary grade span (K–2). Each of its five chapters includes:

Essential Questions with opportunity for reader reflection

Rationale from acknowledged mathematics authorities

Description of the particular step

Examples of the particular step and how to implement it

Development of the step through each of the primary grades

Differentiation strategies

Reader's assignment

Part Two presents guidelines for implementing the balanced math program in kindergarten, grade 1, and grade 2. Included in each of these three chapters are examples specific to that grade, along with practical suggestions for successful implementation.

Part Three offers time management suggestions and responses to frequently asked questions. In addition, we have included, in Chapter 10, recommended guidelines for school leaders to assist them in effectively implementing the five steps within their buildings.

The "Reproducibles" section contains reproducible versions of the templates presented throughout the chapters. These forms can be duplicated for school and classroom use.

As We Begin

We designed *Five Easy Steps to a Balanced Math Program for the Primary Grades* to serve as a road map for classroom teachers in kindergarten and grades 1–2. We encourage you to make this information your own, either by following it to the letter or by adapting it in whatever ways best meet your own individual needs. Our sincere hope is that our model will make you eager to create a balanced math program in your own classroom! If you have any questions along the way, please do not hesitate to contact either of us at the addresses provided in the "About the Authors" section. Ready? Let's get started!

PART ONE

The Five Easy Steps

Step 1: Computational Skills
(Math Review and Mental Math)

Essential Questions

In what ways are you helping students retain math concepts and skills they have already been taught?

How are you helping students develop and refine their number sense?

We suggest taking a few minutes of personal reflection time to respond to these questions.

Rationale

Number sense is essential to student success with computational skills. The key to effective practice when learning any new concept or skill is timely and specific feedback. Providing students with a daily opportunity to reflect on their progress increases their responsibility for learning. Helping students become aware of their individual mistakes or misunderstandings increases their chance for math success.

Teachers also benefit from the practice of regularly reviewing and assessing students' computational skills. They become aware of students' common mistakes and misunderstandings so that they can appropriately modify and adjust instruction. They learn to emphasize computational skills that are meaning-based (making sense) rather than procedure-based (following formulas Withlittle or no understanding).

Description of Step 1: Math Review Component

The first key component of a balanced math program is a simple system for reviewing basic computational skills on a daily basis; we call it "Math Review." During the first 20 minutes of every math class, students solve and process a set of three to five problems. These problems should:

Represent the specific standards for that grade level

Provide practice in several math standards or strands

Match the conceptual focus of the current instructional unit or set of lessons

Reinforce prior learning and retention of previously taught concepts and skills

Provide daily practice for the computation sections on district and state assessments

The purpose of Math Review is simply that: *review.* It is not to instruct students on new concepts and skills. However, regular review of and practice with basic concepts and skills, prior to formal instruction on those concepts and skills (described in Step 3: Conceptual Understanding), greatly enhance student understanding when these *are* taught during a focused set of lessons or unit of study later in the school year.

Math Review is the place in the math hour to discuss with students reasonableness of answer and estimation. It is also the perfect opportunity to help students develop computational strategies and skills. Instead of teaching students a procedure that implies there is only one way to solve a problem, emphasize and model *multiple* approaches to solving problems. This fosters students' mathematical reasoning and develops their number sense. According to Marilyn Burns, nationally recognized mathematics authority, "Number sense encompasses a wide range of abilities, including being able to make reasonable estimates, think and reason flexibly, make sound numerical judgments, and see numbers as useful. Students with number sense have good numerical intuition" (1999, p. 408).

A Deliberate Selection of Problems

An effective Math Review session involves more than simply writing a different set of random arithmetic problems on the board each day. Instead, the teacher deliberately selects specific problems representing different math standards and then focuses student review and practice on variations of those same problems throughout the week. While students practice solving those problems each day, they receive additional guidance and instruction as needed from both the teacher and their peers.

If we want students to maximize their learning of particular math computational skills, we must avoid introducing them to new kinds of problems within the same week. It is far more effective to keep students focused on a few *types* of problems and then have students consistently practice those same types of problems until they learn how to do them.

Math Review establishes a deliberate progression of mathematical concepts and computational skills that increase in difficulty throughout the school year. Problems of the same type recur week after week until the majority of the class learns them. Only then does the teacher introduce a new type of problem to replace the

> *Math Review establishes a deliberate progression of mathematical concepts and computational skills that increase in difficulty throughout the school year.*

one that students have sufficiently learned. In this way, new types of problems are cycled through Math Review as the year proceeds.

If students need to revisit any concepts or skills at some point later in the year, those types of problems can again be included in Math Review. However, if students practice a particular computational concept or skill until they thoroughly understand it, teachers will find that they seldom need to completely re-teach that concept or skill in the future. They can better build on students' prior understanding when those concepts and skills appear again in more challenging problems or applications.

The Math Review Template

The Math Review Template shown in Figure 1.1 is an organizational structure we developed to implement this daily computational practice. It consists of three to five labeled boxes with a problem and accompanying work space in each. These problems target the current math concepts or skills the teacher wants students to focus on during that week. Often teachers include a bonus problem for early finishers, who often need an additional challenge. This bonus problem can be either a word problem that takes one or two steps to solve, or it can be a more difficult version of one of the regular Math Review problems.

For example, the sample primary-grades template shown in Figure 1.1 targets five different math standards or focus topics. The sections that follow explain how we instruct students to solve these problems, as well as how we process the problems together after students have solved them. (*Note:* Specific examples of the Math Review template for kindergarten, grade 1, and grade 2 are

Description of Step 1: Math Review Component

Sample Primary-Grades Math Review Template	Figure 1.1

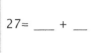

27= ___ + ___	7 + 6 = ___	20 - 8 = _____	 Write the fraction.	___ days = 2 weeks ___ min. =1 hr. ___ in. = 1 ft.
Place Value/ Counting	Addition	Subtraction	Part-Whole Relationship	Measurement

provided in Part Two, "Inside the Primary Classroom." Problems that are more appropriate for each individual grade level appear there.)

Math Review Progression through Primary Grade Span

For the primary grade span, we recommend the following progression for introducing and developing students' number sense through Math Review.

In kindergarten, the process is very teacher-directed and delivered through whole-group instruction. The teacher usually presents three problems to be solved. Students respond orally and show their understanding using manipulatives and through pictures or drawings. Rather than giving students a written quiz to determine student understanding, teachers assess student progress informally.

In first grade, the process at the *beginning* of the school year is also very teacher-directed. Students typically solve three problems, guided by the teacher, and begin to record their written answers on paper. As the year progresses, the teacher can add one or two

Step 1: Computational Skills
(Math Review and Mental Math)

The teacher is critical to the success of Math Review. Students need to hear the teacher giving such encouragement as, "Math Review is a time for practice."

more problems to be solved and encourage students to work more independently. Students can also begin to reflect on their performance, noting what they understand and what they do not. The teacher may decide to assess student understanding a bit more formally, by means of a written quiz covering the same types of problems that the students have practiced all week.

In second grade, the teacher may also begin the year with three Math Review problems, but soon increases the number of problems to five. Students regularly reflect on their progress, especially after reviewing their results on the weekly Math Review Quiz (described later in this chapter).

The Teacher's Role During Math Review

The teacher is critical to the success of Math Review. Students need to hear the teacher giving such encouragement as, "Math Review is a time for *practice*. We are all trying to get better at this, so let's help each other as much as possible."

While the students are working, the teacher circulates throughout the classroom and helps students individually, or invites those who are having difficulty with a particular problem to come forward to the board for individual or small-group assistance. Students can come and go after each problem, depending on their needs. These changing, informal groups, called *flex groups,* provide a safe place for students to seek the help they might otherwise not ask for. The teacher strives to create a collaborative atmosphere in which kids are willing to risk and admit their need for help. The message is: "Learning is a process that begins with *not* knowing. As we practice and help each other, we come to understand."

Processing Math Review

When the time for students to solve the Math Review problems (usually 10 minutes) has elapsed, the teacher and students correct the problems together. The processing of the Math Review problems should take approximately 5 to 10 minutes. The key to processing Math Review effectively is to emphasize number sense and reasonableness of answer and to do this *on a regular (daily) basis.* Processing Math Review helps students determine for themselves whether their own answers are reasonable and make sense. Children in kindergarten through grade 2 need to develop number-sense strategies, rather than merely learn procedural methods. The daily processing of the Math Review problems greatly assists them in doing so.

Teachers who strive to create a classroom climate in which mistakes are regarded as a normal part of the learning process make it much easier for students to want to improve. Students become more receptive to learning how to do an error analysis of their work when their Math Review answers are incorrect. This *error analysis* is a way to help students (1) identify the part of the problem done correctly and (2) pinpoint the part of the problem where they made an error. With this kind of daily practice in analyzing their math processes, students gain confidence in their mathematical ability and *do* improve.

When introducing a new concept or skill into the Math Review mix of problems, or when a majority of the class seems stuck on a particular problem, the teacher may lead the class through the step-by-step computational procedure, pointing out the critical elements and asking students for a reasonable answer. The teacher

What is most important in the processing of Math Review is teaching students how to conduct their own error analysis.

emphasizes the key points and encourages students to verbalize how they will use those key points to solve the problem from then on. As students develop their ability to write, teachers model for them how to take notes on key points. This helps students remember how to solve such a problem on their own the next time they encounter a similar one.

Let's revisit the five sample problems illustrated in Figure 1.1 to describe how teachers can effectively process each one. Figure 1.2 shows an expansion of the Math Review problems with key processing points pertaining to each one.

Other Important Ways to Process Math Review

When introducing students to the processing of Math Review, we recommend that the teacher direct the process (as described earlier in this chapter) until students are familiar with the way it is done and can begin to use the process independently. However, there are several other ways to process Math Review and to conduct an error analysis; these are described in the following subsections. Note that these different ways are offered so that teachers can vary the way they process Math Review. Our intent is not to suggest that each teacher use each and every way presented every single day. Math Review should be fun, not overwhelming! These are merely different methods to effectively develop students' number sense. The teacher should select the methods that best meet the changing needs of the class. What is most important in the processing of Math Review is teaching students how to conduct their own error analysis. Teachers play a critical role in consistently modeling this process.

Student-Directed.   In this method, student volunteers explain to the class the procedure they followed to arrive at a solution to each of the Math Review problems. If other students

Description of Step 1: Math Review Component

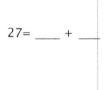

$$27 = \_\_\_ + \_\_\_$$

Place Value/ Counting

$$7 + 6 = \_\_\_\_\_$$

Addition

$$20 - 8 = \_\_\_\_\_$$

Subtraction

Write the fraction.

Part-Whole Relationship

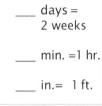

___ days = 2 weeks

___ min. = 1 hr.

___ in. = 1 ft.

Measurement

Place Value Counting

Key Points

- What makes up 27?
  How many groups of ten, and how many ones?

- Counting: What number comes before 27?
  What number comes after 27? How many more
  to reach 30? What number is 10 more than 27?

Addition

Key Points

Help students develop number-sense strategies.

- Doubles plus one: 6 + 6 + 1 = 13

- Doubles less one: 7 + 7 = 14 - 1 = 13

- Place value: 13 is 1 ten and 3 ones or 13 ones

Subtraction

Key Points

Help students develop number-sense strategies
before overemphasizing procedural solution.

- Build up through 10: 8 + 2 = 10, 10 + 10 = 20;
  2 + 10 = 12; answer is 12

- Think addition: 8 + ___ = 20; answer is 12

- Reasonable answer: 20   10   10

Note: A reasonable answer gives students a way
to judge the effectiveness of a strategy they are
trying (e.g., "My answer should be close to 10.").

Part-Whole Relationship

Key Points

- How many pieces make up the whole?

- How many pieces are shaded?

- Here is how we write the fraction for this
  picture ($\frac{1}{3}$).

Note: Understanding of the operations with
fractions taught in upper grades depends on students
understanding the part-whole relationship.

Measurement

Key Points

- This kind of problem is important to help
  young students have daily experience with
  measurement.

- These items are considered general
  knowledge/life skills (e.g., relative size and
  length) and students' understanding of these
  types of problems typically depends on their
  background knowledge.

- This formatting is typical of that used on
  high-stakes state assessments (e.g., "___days
  2 weeks," instead of "How many days in
  1 week?").

Real-life application: During the processing of this
problem, ask students: "Name something that is
about 1 foot in length," "Name something that
lasts about an hour," and so on.

used different approaches to reach the same solution, and the teacher decides it would benefit the rest of the class to see and/or hear them, the teacher may invite those students to share their approaches as well.

"Pass the Pen." This is a diagnostic tool we use when most of the students know how to do a particular kind of problem. It is an effective method to assist the teacher in seeing where students might have trouble with a particular part of a problem and to provide needed instruction. As one student demonstrates one step of the solution on the board or overhead projector, others watch to see if they agree or disagree. The student at the board then "passes the pen" (or marker, or chalk) to another student who must demonstrate the next step. This continues until the problem is solved and all agree that the answer is correct.

Speedy System. When students have become successful with the Math Review problems, volunteers go to the board and just write the answer to the problem. They then ask the class, "How many agree? How many disagree?" This enables the class to determine quickly whether or not their answers are correct.

Row or Group Expert. The first student to finish in a studentrow or cooperative group begins to assist other students in that row or cooperative group with the day's assigned problems. During this time, the "expert" discusses solutions with other students in that row or group who have also completed the problems. Such conversations prove very helpful for students who have not yet mastered the concepts being presented.

Row or Group Representative. Assign each row or cooperative group of students a certain problem that they must

Description of Step 1: Math Review Component

solve and reach consensus on. After all students have completed the day's problems, the row or cooperative group representative shares with the class the group's answer to the assigned problem and describes how his or her group determined its answer.

Math Vocabulary. Encourage students to use related math vocabulary and write related number sentences next to the problems as they are solved and later shared with the whole class. Teachers often create a Math Word Wall of frequently used math vocabulary to assist students in incorporating correct mathematical terms into their oral and written work.

Identify Math Concepts. Ask students to identify key math concepts they are practicing in given problems. For example, if students are extending a pattern such as 2, 4, 6, 8, . . . , they may not realize that they are working with the concept of pattern unless the teacher deliberately asks them to identify the particular math concept as "patterns."

Common Mistake. Alert students to the most common mistake made on a particular problem, to help them avoid that mistake from then on. For example, first- or second-grade studentsoften forget to regroup in a subtraction problem such as 23 14. Rather than regroup one of the tens into 10 ones, add those 10 ones to the 3 ones, and then subtract the 4 from 13, they will simply subtract 4 from 3 and 1 from 2 to write 11 as the answer.

One cautionary note: Math Review provides such stimulating opportunities for teacher instruction and student learning that it can easily expand to encompass the entire time allocated for math! A way to prevent this is to focus the Math Review processing on only two or three problems at first, and vary that focus each day.

Encourage students to use related math vocabulary and write related number sentences next to the problems as they are solved and later shared with the whole class.

In this way, students will develop their number sense and conceptual understanding underlying the procedures, as well as reflect on their own learning; at the same time, the teacher will be able to stay within the recommended 20 to 25 minutes allotted to Math Review *and* Mental Math (described later in this chapter).

In the beginning of the year, or whenever teachers introduce any new process to students, the time required is naturally longer. However, strive to limit step 1 to about one-third of the total math session. Otherwise, the first step in your balanced math program will unbalance the other four!

Assessment: The Math Review Quiz

Essential Questions

How will you know if Math Review is effective?

*How will you assess **for** learning (gather information about student mistakes and misconceptions in order to differentiate instruction)?*

Rationale

Regular assessment of student progress is necessary to make Math Review effective. If students are to improve, teachers need insights regarding student misconceptions. Formative assessment results provide teachers with diagnostic information on a regular basis. Teachers use these results to differentiate instruction that should include intervention for struggling learners and enrichment or acceleration for more able learners. To know what instructional

Assessment: The Math Review Quiz

changes they need to make to meet the learning needs of all students, teachers administer a Math Review Quiz every week.

The weekly Math Review Quiz provides teachers with the means to determine which students do and do not understand the computational problems they have been practicing throughout the week. It provides both teachers *and* students with timely feedback and allows the children the opportunity to reflect on their current performance, so as to plan for personal improvement. Again, the value of this weekly assessment is that it is *formative*. If students do not demonstrate proficiency on certain items, teachers need to decide what they must do to assist students to solve them correctly.

This analysis of student results may also reveal the need for the teacher to remove particular types of problems from the daily Math Review and place them in the instructional component of a current or future math lesson. Remember, the purpose of Math Review is *review*—it is not intended for direct instruction. Alternatively, analyzing the results of the Math Review Quiz may reveal that the *types* of problems are appropriate, but the particular problems are too difficult for the majority of the students to solve independently. This adjustment can be made immediately to make the problems more accessible to students. In both cases, such formative assessment is used to *inform* instruction.

The Math Review Quiz

Kindergarten teachers may not regard a weekly quiz as appropriate for their young students. However, they certainly are able to assess students informally to determine student proficiency with the types of problems they are presenting daily during Math Review. The Math Review Quiz as described here typically becomes

The weekly Math Review Quiz provides teachers with the means to determine which students do and donot understand the computational problems they have been practicing throughout the week.

Step 1: Computational Skills
(Math Review and Mental Math)

The Math Review Quiz consists of two problems for each of the three to five kinds of problems practiced during the preceding four days.

a weekly assessment of students' computational understanding beginning at some point in grade 1. The decision as to when students are ready to complete a quiz independently should be made by individual teachers or grade-level teams. We present the information here so that teachers can reference it when appropriate.

The Math Review Quiz consists of two problems for each of the three to five kinds of problems practiced during the preceding four days. The reason for using two problems per concept or skill is diagnostic: If a student incorrectly solves one problem but gets the other one right, the teacher may determine that the student simply made a calculation error. If the student misses both problems, the teacher correctly interprets this as indicating a need for further instruction on that particular concept or skill. This weekly assessment enables the teacher to differentiate daily instruction for students according to student need.

To be considered proficient, students need to correctly solve nearly all of the problems on the Math Review Quiz. Students who can demonstrate this level of proficiency on the quiz may, during the following week, choose to do only the bonus problem provided daily, or to assist other students by acting as tutors or helpers. However, these students must take the following week's quiz to show that they can still correctly solve these same kinds of problems. Once new types of problems are cycled in, all students should complete the daily Math Review practice problems.

A Sample Math Review Quiz

Figure 1.3 is an example of a Math Review Quiz that matches the five-problem Math Review sample given in Figure 1.1. There are two problems for each type of problem the students practiced during the daily Math Review.

Sample Math Review Quiz	Figure 1.3

1. 36 = _____ + _____

2. 57 = _____ + _____

3. 7 + 6 = _____

4. 9 + 8 = _____

5. 30 - 9 = _____

6. 40 - 8 = _____

7. Draw $\dfrac{3}{4}$

8. Draw $\dfrac{2}{3}$

9. _____ days = 3 weeks

10. _____ in. = 2 ft.

Scoring the Math Review Quiz

It is important that students receive immediate and specific feedback regarding their performance on the Math Review Quiz. Although first-grade teachers usually score the papers themselves, an effective method for providing immediate feedback to students is to have them correct their own quizzes as soon as they are able to do so. Using a red marking pen, students star an answer if correct and check it if incorrect. In this way, they can see firsthand where they are doing well and where they need to improve.

Math Review Quiz Self-Reflection

Primary-grade students can be shown how to reflect on their progress. With teacher guidance, kindergarten children can think about and say which problems they know how to do in Math Review and which ones they need help with. First-grade students can think and say what they will try to improve upon in the next week's Math Review problems. Second-grade students can score their own papers and, next to the problems missed, write a phrase about why they missed that particular problem. They can then turn over their papers to write a brief self-reflection that addresses their current Math Review Quiz performance, along with a simple plan for improvement during the next week. *Note:* Teachers of special education students with writing challenges and English-language learners can follow these guidelines by asking students to reflect orally on their performance. As soon as students are able to write independently, however, we do ask them to complete their self-reflection as described here.

The effectiveness of this self-reflection process depends on the classroom teacher emphasizing the appropriate use of student errors and misunderstandings during the Math Review processing each day. As teachers help students begin to see errors as providing important information to know about their learning process—an assessment *for* learning—instead of being a negative reflection of their mathematical ability, students improve their performance. This active self-reflection helps learners focus on personal goals for improvement just before they begin a new week of Math Review.

Tutors and Tutees

Another successful method we use to build a supportive classroom atmosphere and meet the varying needs of all students is "Tutors and Tutees," a student– student partnership so named by Scott Koopsen, a teacher from Carlsbad, California. The *tutors* are peer helpers who volunteer to provide assistance to other students during Math Review, at recess, or even during lunch; the *tutees* are students who are struggling with one or more computational skills as indicated either by their daily Math Review practice sessions and/or their performance on the weekly Math Review Quiz. To become eligible to be a tutor, a student must correctly solve nearly all of the problems on the quiz. If there are 10 problems, for example, students must score at least 8 out of 10. During the following week, these students may then assist other students (the tutees) who scored lower than eight during the Math Review daily practice. However, *all* students must take the next Math Review Quiz.

Very often students can learn computational strategies more effectively from their peers than from their teachers. Having tutors work with tutees also provides teachers with needed assistance when many students ask for help at the same time. Because the teacher has organized Math Review to take advantage of students' ability to assist one another, students who need help get it when they need it, and thus are less likely to continue struggling unaided as the year progresses.

A word of caution is needed here, however. It is important to challenge tutors who can successfully solve the Math Review problems to do *more advanced* work, rather than just assist other students week after week. Even though they certainly gain great benefits by coaching or teaching other students, students who are proficient at Math Review must also be encouraged to tackle problems that challenge them mathematically. The daily bonus problem that accompanies the regular Math Review problems closely relates to the computational focus of the five problems the class is practicing during any given week, but it should be more rigorous and extend student understanding of one or more of those kinds of problems.

The Home Connection and Extra Practice

Kindergarten and first-grade students should take home daily Math Review problems for parents to review so that they can provide their children with additional help wherever needed. Once students begin taking Math Review Quizzes, students instead take home their evaluated quizzes for parents to review and sign. This weekly accountability informs parents of the actual progress their child is making in math computation. If students score less than 80%, parents can help them practice problems like those missed on the quiz.

To assist the parents in doing this, teachers typically send home practice problems to be completed for homework. The next morning, the teacher quickly checks to see if students have completed and returned the practice problems. By consistently monitoring the completion of this extra practice, the teacher communicates high expectations to both students and parents and establishes a standard of accountability.

During Math Review, the teacher works with these same students one-on-one or in a small flex group to make sure they receive additional instruction and assistance. This combined effort—the teacher's extra help during Math Review and the parents' help at home—has proven quite successful for students who struggle with computation.

For certain students, help at home is not possible or not available. To respond to this reality, we pair these students with peers, parent volunteers, or teacher aides who help them practice at school. Depending on the unique circumstances at each school, the teachers and administrators must establish their own internal support system for helping these students before, during, and/or after the regular school day.

Benefits of the Math Review Quiz

The Math Review Quiz provides the teacher with a weekly formative assessment that:

Identifies students who need remediation or intervention

Identifies students who need enrichment or acceleration

Gauges the effectiveness of computational instruction

If only a few students score below 80% on the weekly quiz, those children can be taught individually or in small groups until they improve. If a majority of the class falls below the 80% score, the teacher needs to reevaluate student understanding during Math Review and to make instructional adjustments accordingly. In this way, assessment serves its most important function, that of informing instruction.

Examples of weekly Math Review Quizzes aligned to daily Math Review problems are included in the specific grade-level implementation chapters of Part Two.

If a majority of the class falls below the 80% score, the teacher needs to reevaluate student understanding during Math Review and to make instructional adjustments accordingly.

Differentiation

The following are general guidelines and suggestions for meeting the diverse learning needs of students at various ability levels within the classroom. Certain of these suggestions have been described throughout this chapter. However, we have included them again here along with additional strategies.

Flexible Grouping.   Using the data from the weekly Math Review Quiz or from informal observation and assessment, teachers create small student "flex groups." Place those students who continually have difficulty during Math Review into a group that will receive daily help from the teacher. As individual students start experiencing success in Math Review or begin to demonstrate their improved understanding on the Math Review Quiz, have them rejoin the class as a whole to work independently. Other students in need of direct assistance from the teacher can join the group until such time as they too are able to work successfully on their own.

Peer Assistance. Match students who show success on Math Review (tutors or helpers) with students who are struggling. During daily Math Review, these student pairs work together to complete the problems. Encourage the use of appropriate manipulatives to assist struggling students to understand the particular concepts and skills that are causing difficulty.

Bonus Problem. Each day, provide students who are already proficient at the concepts and skills being presented with a bonus problem that involves more difficult mathematics. Teachers often include a sixth box on the Math Review template for a daily bonus

Differentiation

problem. This bonus problem can be either a word problem or a more challenging version of any one of the five regular problems. The bonus problem engages students who finish the regular problems before others. It is also an excellent way to differentiate instruction for students who are ready for more advanced conceptsor skills.

English-Language Learners. Provide students who are learning English with peer assistance, and emphasize vocabulary development during the processing of the Math Review problems. Post key mathematical vocabulary in the classroom on a Math WordWall. Emphasize vocabulary during the daily practice of Mental Math (as described in the next section), and include writing

during Math Review on a daily basis.

Error Analysis (Teacher). Keep track of the concepts that are most problematic for students. Emphasize those conceptsrepeatedly during Math Review processing activities, as well as during Mental Math.

Individual Assistance. Find times during the day to offer struggling students one-on-one assistance. This may include meeting with these students before or after school, during lunch,or during breaks. Even a few minutes of individual work with a student can make a huge difference in that student's mathematical understanding.

Description of Step 1: Mental Math Component

Essential Questions

How are you providing students daily mental practice with number sense?

How are you providing opportunities for students to develop their own strategies for doing math problems in their heads?

Rationale

Students need regular opportunities to develop effective computational strategies that are based on number sense. Helping students use number strategies that they find comfortable and accurate is an effective way to develop number sense. Students need daily mental practice to develop and retain strong number sense and effective computational skills.

Cathy L. Seeley, president of the National Council of Teachers of Mathematics (NCTM), in her December 2005 "President's Message" to members, emphasizes the importance of learning to compute mentally:

> *In my observation, mental math does not receive the attentionit deserves. Perhaps this is because the development of mental techniques is not always explicitly stated as an objective or state-level standard. Whatever the reason, the time has come to invest in helping students build the mental math skills in their tool kits as part of their comprehensive mathematical understanding. The payoff for this investment can be tremendous both in improving students' mathematical abilities and in giving a visible sign that we are committed to preparing students with the kind of mathematical proficiency that the public can readily appreciate.*

Description of Step 1: Mental Math Component

How to Implement Mental Math

The second part of step 1 is Mental Math, a three-problem, computational workout for the brain that students love doing. Mental Math takes about five minutes of class time and immediately follows the processing of the Math Review problems. However, teachers report that they have found other times during the school day in which to allow students to practice Mental Math. Such times include lining up for recess, restroom, or lunch; transition times between subjects; walking from the classroom to special area classes; and so on.

The purpose of Mental Math is to provide students with *mental* practice in computing basic number facts and combining mathematical operations. The teacher selects a particular math theme or combination of themes and then dictates a string of numbers and operations that students compute mentally to determine the final answer.

Typical themes for Mental Math in the primary grades include:

One more/one less than a given number

Counting by twos, fives, and tens

Anchors of 5 and 10 (five-frame and ten-frame)

Doubles

Part-part-whole relationships (fact-family groups)

Number facts (addition and subtraction)

Math vocabulary

Measurement concepts (time, money, calendar, inches, feet, etc.)

> *The purpose of Mental Math is to provide students with* mental *practice in computing basic number facts and combining mathematical operations.*

After selecting one or more themes for Mental Math, the teacher then prepares a corresponding number string to dictate orally to the class. For example, to help students practice understanding the themes of one more, one less, and doubles, the teacher could prepare and dictate the following number string:

Start with one more than five (6); double that number (12); think what is one less than that number (11).

Pause briefly after each operational step. At each pause, students have a chance to calculate mentally before the teacher moves on to the next step, but they do not write anything down until the final answer. In the example, students calculate the answer in their heads and write "11" (we hope!) in their math journals right beneath the Math Review problems of the day.

The answer is not given yet, however. The teacher repeats the same problem to allow students who might need a second chance to succeed. Those children who think they know the correct answer are asked to calculate again "just to make sure." The teacher then asks the students to say the answer aloud together. The answer is verified by computing the problem aloud in increments to help those remaining students who still were unable to do it. In this way, everyone stays involved. By keeping everyone engaged in this way, the teacher helps students see how the answer was determined, and encourages those who are struggling to try the next problem.

Classes can usually accomplish three Mental Math problems in five minutes once students are familiar with the procedure. Choose the number of problems that is appropriate for your class and

Description of Step 1: Mental Math Component

available time. Use problems that are fairly easy when first introducing this activity to the children. You can make the problems more challenging as the year progresses and your students' confidence and ability improve.

Students often want to create their own Mental Math problems to dictate to the rest of the class. We always encourage this kind of involvement. However, before allowing these volunteers to say their problems aloud, students must write out the number string and have the teacher check it for appropriateness of difficulty (often student-created strings are too long and convoluted). We have also found it a good practice to write down the problem before saying it aloud. More than once, we've been unable to repeat the number string exactly, causing a minor uproar in the classroom!

A teacher in Louisiana came up with a wonderful way to engage students in learning math vocabulary terms while practicing Mental Math problems. She writes a new math term, with its definition, on a sentence strip and places that sentence strip some-where on the wall in her classroom. For example, to introduce the term *dozen,* she writes on the strip, "One dozen   12 units." During Mental Math that day, she incorporates that term in her number string like this: "Start with a dozen; subtract half a dozen; . . . " and so on. Each day or two she introduces a new math vocabulary term in the same way. During the *Five Easy Steps* workshop, she reported that her students began coming into class each morning looking for the new math term, knowing that she would use it that day during Mental Math. In this ingenious way, the teacher motivated her students to learn new math vocabulary; for them, it became a fun kind of game.

Mental Math Benefits

Practice doesn't always make perfect, but doing Mental Math daily throughout the school year helps all students achieve dramatic improvement. It provides students with regular opportunities to apply properties and patterns of our number system.

Many excellent commercial sources for Mental Math are available, but we find that teachers and students alike enjoy making them up themselves once they become familiar with the process. Sample Mental Math problems are included in each of the kindergarten, grade 1, and grade 2 implementation chapters to provide readers with a model for doing so.

Reader's Assignment

Rather than waiting until the end of this book to begin planning how to implement these suggestions for creating a balanced math program in your own classroom, you may wish to put this information to use immediately and plan as you go. We have therefore included a Reader's Assignment at the end of each of the five steps to guide you (and your grade-level or teaching colleagues) through the step-by-step process of planning your own balanced program.

Reader's Assignment

Plan your own grade-level Math Review template, sample Math Review problems, and sample Mental Math problems. Refer to your particular classroom chapter (kindergarten, grade 1, or grade 2) in Part Two. Examples in these grade-specific chapters will assist you in planning your first daily Math Review problems, Mental Math problems, and Math Review Quizzes. Refer also to Chapter 9 for answers to frequently asked questions about step 1, Computational Skills (Math Review and Mental Math).

Step 1 Products

Create a Math Review template for your grade level

Include sample Math Review problems

Prepare a sample Math Review Quiz

Create a sample Mental Math problem appropriate for your grade level

Consider

What plans do you have for implementing Math Review and Mental Math?

Number of days per week?

Number of problems?

Template you will use?

Assessment or Math Review Quiz you will give?

Next steps you will take?

Step 2: Problem Solving

CHAPTER 2

Essential Questions

How are you providing opportunities for students to apply and explain their mathematical reasoning?

How are you including writing in your math program?

Rationale

The National Council of Teachers of Mathematics' *Principles and Standards for School Mathematics* (2000) states that students should be able to:

Organize and consolidate their mathematical thinking through communication

Communicate mathematical thinking coherently and clearly to others

Analyze and evaluate the mathematical thinking and strategies of others

Use the language of mathematics to express mathematical ideas precisely

Marilyn Burns emphasizes the chief benefits that both students and teachers realize when writing is incorporated into mathematics:

> *Writing in math class supports learning because it requires students to organize, clarify, and reflect on their ideas—all useful processes for making sense of mathematics. In addition,*

Step 2: Problem Solving

when students write, their papers provide a window into their understandings, their misconceptions, and their feelings about the content they're learning (2004, p. 30).

In the same article, Burns shares key strategies teachers can use to incorporate writing (2004, p. 33):

1. Establish the purposes of writing in math class.

2. Establish yourself (the teacher) as the audience.

3. Ask students to include details and to explain their thinking as thoroughly as possible.

4. Post useful mathematics vocabulary.

5. Have students share their writing in pairs or small groups.

Problem solving gives students opportunities to *apply* their math skills and concepts. Student writing also provides diagnostic information for the teacher. As students develop experience with problem solving, they gain confidence and experience success.

The problem-solving step of a balanced math program provides students with a dual opportunity:

1. To apply the mathematics they are learning in the Conceptual Understanding Unit of instruction (described in step 3) to a problem-solving situation

2. To communicate their mathematical thinking to others

Mathematics and language processes are interrelated. Our underlying purpose in asking students to communicate their thinking in both oral and written forms is to teach students how to explain their *process* to others. In doing this, students develop the ability to think logically and follow the sequence of mental steps needed to solve math-related problems in real life.

We recognize that some students automatically compute mentally and are able to arrive at the answer quite quickly. Often, though, when teachers ask these students how they solved the problem, the reply is, "I just figured it out in my head" or "My brain told me." Other students are never quite sure how to approach a problem if it is not already in an arithmetic format. Because our goal is to produce mathematically powerful students who can reason, solve, and explain both procedural and application problems, we need to set up learning experiences through which students become able to articulate the mathematical process they followed—first for themselves, then for others.

Description of Step 2

Selecting the Problem-Solving Task

In the first stage of developing students' problem-solving skills, we introduce students to the *process* of mathematically showing how to solve a complex word problem requiring more than one step. The Problem-Solving Task gives students the opportunity to practice doing this. The task is a carefully selected problem matched to the current instructional unit or set of lessons that students discuss, solve, and write about during one or more class sessions.

When selecting a particular problem for students to solve, we look for one that will allow them to demonstrate their ability to apply the math they are learning to a real-world problem or situation. To assist us in doing this, we refer to the guiding questions listed on the next page.

Does this problem promote application of the mathematical ideas presented in the current instructional focus or unit of study?

Does this problem match students' current instructional level?

Is this problem accessible to all students?

Is the problem relevant and engaging to students?

Does this problem require students to "stretch" their mathematical reasoning abilities?

Does this problem involve more than one strand or standard of mathematics?

Is there more than one way to solve the problem?

Could the problem be extended or enriched?

Do *I* fully understand the mathematics in this problem, so that I can better facilitate student understanding?

With these guiding questions in mind, teachers can use the problem-solving resources provided in their math textbook series and supplemental math resource materials to select worthwhile mathematical tasks for students. Many excellent sources for problem-solving tasks are now available online (in particular, mathforum.org). Please refer to the math Webliography provided in the "References and Other Resources" section at the end of this book. In addition, we recommend *Nonfiction Writing Prompts for Math, Lower Elementary* (Ruthven, 2005), one of the books in the Write to Know series from Advanced Learning Press.

Teaching Students to Solve the Problem-Solving Task

Once we select the problem that will become the Problem-Solving Task, we follow a specific instructional sequence to teach students how to mathematically solve an application problem and communicate orally and in writing the process they used. Our ultimate goal for primary-grade students is for them to be able— *by the end of the school year*—to solve independently a two-step or a multistep problem and to communicate verbally (kindergarten) and in writing (grade 1 and grade 2) the process they used.

With that goal in mind, we first model the process for the whole class until students are familiar with the steps. Next, we have students solve the selected problem in cooperative groups or teams. Once they are able to do this, we partner students to solve the given problem together. Lastly, we expect students to be able to complete the entire process independently. In the following subsections, we describe each of these stages in more detail.

Whole-Class Instruction. The teacher first introduces the Problem-Solving Task to the class and helps students understand its connection to the current instructional unit focus. He or she then guides students to solve the problem using words, pictures, and/or numbers. Here is a sequence of suggested steps for doing just that:

1. Teacher and students read the problem together. The teacher makes sure that students understand what the problem is asking.

2. Students take 5 to 10 minutes to attempt to solve the problem individually, using manipulatives if appropriate.

3. Students record their individual work on paper.

Our ultimate goal for primary-grade students is for them to be able to solve independently a two-step or a multistep problem and to communicate verbally and in writing the process they used.

4. Students share possible strategies for solving the problem.

5. Teacher and students decide on a solution to the problem.

6. Teacher creates a class *Data Sheet* (a chart showing all the work done to solve the problem, usually represented in words, pictures, and/or numbers).

7. Students copy the class Data Sheet.

8. Teachers and students compose a few sentences to describe how the problem was solved.

9. Teacher records the sentences on chart paper to be posted in the classroom.

10. Students copy the class-written explanation.

Cooperative Teams.   Once students are familiar with the problem-solving process just described, the teacher arranges students into small, cooperative groups or teams. Guided by the teacher, students attempt to solve a new problem—without teacher assistance. Using words, pictures, and/or numbers, the students complete a Data Sheet (again, our term for the work students do to solve the problem) and then copy their work onto easel-size chart paper. The members of the group then share the team's solutions with the rest of the class. The group members explain the process they followed and try to convince the class that their answer is correct and makes sense. Different teams will describe their processes differently and thus add to everyone's understanding of how to solve the problem. The class and teacher then discuss the different solutions presented and determine the actual answer.

This reporting activity enables the teacher to provide further instructions as to how the Data Sheet is to be done and to respond to student questions. This modeling is critical to ensuring students' long-term understanding and success on the second part of the process, the Problem-Solving Task Write-Up (described in the next section).

Once the presentations are finished, students display their chart-paper posters on the board or around the classroom as examples of their cooperative team problem solving. They will later refer to these models to assist them in completing subsequent Data Sheets for new problems. Teachers exchange existing posters for new ones each time the class completes a new Problem-Solving Task. This maintains student interest in problem solving all year long.

The Problem-Solving Task Write-Up Guide. Because we want students eventually to be able to communicate their mathematical process in writing, we now provide them with a format for doing so. The Problem-Solving Task Write-Up Guide establishes an organized structure through which students explain the mathematical work they have represented on their group Data Sheets. A sample write-up guide that includes the directions for both the Data Sheet and the written explanation is shown in Figure 2.1. Teachers can use this template or create their own, depending on the grade and ability levels of their students. Note that certain instructions may not be developmentally appropriate for all K–2 children (i.e., write a short paragraph). Use as many of the directions as your students can accomplish and add the remaining ones when it is appropriate to do so. However, we suggest teaching children who are not yet writing to use the same transition words (*first, next, then, after that, finally*) orally when they explain their math process. Familiarization with and verbal use of these transition words will help children express their understanding on paper when they are ready to begin writing out their math steps.

> *The Problem-Solving Task Write-Up Guide establishes an organized structure through which students explain the mathematical work they have represented on their group Data Sheets.*

Figure 2.1	Problem-Solving Task Write-Up Guide (Primary Grades)

PROBLEM-SOLVING TASK WRITE-UP GUIDE: PRIMARY

Directions:

1. Write your name on a piece of paper.
2. Solve the problem using words, pictures, and/or numbers.
3. Number each step as you work to solve the problem.
4. Write a number sentence to match your problem.
5. Write your answer in a sentence under your solution.
6. Now write a short paragraph that explains, step by step, how you solved the problem.
7. Use math vocabulary.
8. Use this write-up guide to help you write your paragraph:

Data Sheet:

Solve the problem using words, pictures, and/or numbers.

Write-Up:

First I_____. Next I _____

_____ . Then I_____.

After that I_____.

Finally, I_____.

Description of Step 2

Here is a very helpful strategy that enables students to more easily transfer their recorded work from the Data Sheet to the write-up guide. Instruct them to number each of their steps as they complete their Data Sheets and then write a corresponding sentence on the write-up guide that describes each numbered step. Model for them how to do this. This simple strategy prevents students from writing: "First I read the problem. Then I thought about it. Next I worked it out. After that, I got my answer. Finally, I showed my answer to the teacher." Instead, their written work describes the actual *math steps* they followed to solve the problem.

Certain problems may not require five sentences to describe the actual math steps (one for each of the listed transition words), or they may require more than five. Instruct students to write as many sentences as they need *according to the numbered steps* on their Data Sheets, using transition words as needed. This will do much to discourage students from trying to arbitrarily fit their math steps into the five-sentence write-up guide format rather than merely using it as a guide for communicating their mathematical process.

Independent Student Work. When the teacher decides that all students have had sufficient modeling, practice, and peer support in completing a Data Sheet and the corresponding write-up in cooperative groups and then with individual partners, he or she assigns a new Problem-Solving Task and asks students to try completing a Data Sheet and corresponding write-up independently. The teacher reviews the work students complete on their own to determine if further clarification and instruction are needed. Once students demonstrate that they understand and can follow the process independently, the teacher can confidently assign a Problem-Solving Task to be completed by students *on their own.*

Step 2: Problem Solving

Regardless of when teachers begin this process with students, the benefits of teaching them how to solve word problems and communicate their processes are significant.

This accomplishes the goal we set earlier in the year: to enable students to do this process independently by the end of the school year. Regardless of when teachers begin this process with students, the benefits of teaching them how to solve word problems and communicate their processes are significant. Regular practice will prepare students for problem-solving success in subsequent grades, in everyday life, and on district and state assessments of their mathematical skills.

Problem-Solving Strategies

The following is a list of strategies that students use to solve word problems:

Guess and check

Act it out

Work backward

Draw a picture

Make a table, chart, or graph

Make a list

Write a number sentence

Use logical reasoning

Find a pattern

To become successful problem solvers, children need practice with these strategies until the strategies become part of students' problem-solving toolkits. A note of caution is appropriate here, however. Most real-life problem-solving situations, and problems that appear on state assessments, do not neatly match one particular strategy from the preceding list. Children need to realize that knowing a *variety* of problem-solving strategies will better equip them to become confident problem solvers who know how to use strategies appropriate to the given situation.

Problem-Solving Steps for Primary Students

This section lists problem-solving steps to share with students. Teachers can make a chart of these to post in the classroom and then follow as a guide when modeling how to solve a word problem. This chart (which appears again in the "Reproducibles" section at the end of this book) can be duplicated for students to keep at school and to take home to parents. As stated earlier, certain steps may not be developmentally appropriate for all primary-grade children, particularly students in kindergarten. Use as many of the directions as your students can understand, and begin including the remaining ones when appropriate. Teaching young students this sequence of steps will lay a strong foundation for their future problem-solving success.

Get Ready to Solve the Problem.

1. Read the problem first.

2. Underline or circle the important facts and key words.

3. What are you supposed to find out?

4. Are there any "tricky" parts to the problem?

5. What math vocabulary words are in the problem?

6. Which math strategies will you use?

7. Do you need manipulatives or other math tools to help you?

Solve the Problem.

1. Solve the problem using words, pictures, and/or numbers.

2. Number each of your problem-solving steps (1, 2, 3, . . .) on your Data Sheet.

3. Write a number sentence to show how you solved the problem.

4. Write your answer in a word sentence after you complete your steps.

5. Check your work to see if it makes sense.

Write How You Solved the Problem.

1. Find the first math step you did on your Data Sheet (the step labeled #1).

2. Complete the sentence starter, "*First I . . .* ", writing what you did first. (This should *not* be: "First I read the problem.")

3. Find the second math step you did on your Data Sheet (the step labeled #2).

4. Complete the sentence starter, "*Next I . . .* ", writing what you did second.

5. Continue this way until you have written a sentence for each of the other numbered math steps. Use other transition words (*then, after that, finally*) to help you.

6. Use math vocabulary in as many sentences as you can.

7. Check each sentence to make sure it describes a *math step*.

8. Check to make sure each sentence makes sense.

Want a Bonus Challenge?

1. Can you add the word *because* after each math step you write and then explain why you did that step?

2. Can you include other math vocabulary words to help explain how you solved the problem?

3. Can you solve the problem in more than one way?

4. Can you find someone who solved it differently than you did?

5. Can you change the problem to make it more challenging?

6. Can you solve your own challenging problem?

7. Can you find someone else who will try to solve your problem?

Figure 2.2 shows an example of a multistep Problem-Solving Task, with an accompanying Data Sheet and write-up, that is appropriate for the primary grades. We chose this problem because it meets the criteria listed in the guiding questions for problem selection (listed earlier in this chapter). Readers will find a Problem-Solving Task appropriate for kindergarten, grade 1, and grade 2 students in Chapters 6, 7, and 8, respectively. In addition, Chapter 9 sets out a weekly teaching schedule that includes a Problem-Solving Task and the other components of our balanced math program model.

Figure 2.2	Problem-Solving Student Work Sample (Primary Grades)

PROBLEM-SOLVING TASK WRITE-UP: PRIMARY

Name _____ **Courtney** _____

> ### Bean Bag Game
> - Ben got 190 points with 2 tosses.
> - Kim got more points than Ben.
> - Show 2 different scores Kim could get.
> - Explain with pictures, numbers, and words:
>   —Why you chose the numbers.
>   —How you found each score.
>
>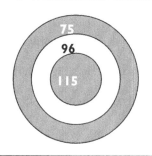

One Score

Pictures	Numbers	Words
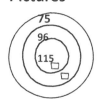	115 + 96 = 211 more than 190.	I just added 115 and 96 and that is

Another Score

Pictures	Numbers	Words
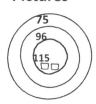	115 + 115 = 230	I took 115 and added 115 and that is more than 190.

How I solved this Problem-Solving Task. First I looked at the picture of the target. Then I drew bean bags in the two highest rings of the target. Next I added those numbers together to see if they were more than Ben's score. After that I drew two bean bags in the highest ring. Finally I added 115 and 115 together and that was higher than Ben's score too.

Source: From the K–7 Math Performance Task Binder. For its use, special thanks to the San Diego County Office of Education and the K–2 Performance Assessment Team. Reprinted with permission from Advanced Learning Press.

An Investment of Time

It is important not to rush the process of teaching students to independently complete the Problem-Solving Task Data Sheet and write-up. A thorough job of initial instruction, combined with sufficient classroom practice, will prevent many future headaches for both teachers and students. While showing students how to correctly complete their first Data Sheets and write-ups, the teacher not only models the correct process for students to follow, but also emphasizes the correct use of mathematical vocabulary, clear mathematical reasoning, and verification of solution.

The goal of step 2 in a balanced math program is to demonstrate for students how to communicate their mathematical understanding by following a specific format and using a specific procedure for doing so. If teachers invest the time needed to teach their students to truly understand and apply this process, they will see wonderful results for their efforts: students who can apply mathematical concepts and procedures to real-world situations.

Suggested Problem-Solving Sequence for Grades K–2

It is essential that students experience initial and continuing success with problem solving if they are to develop confidence in their mathematical reasoning ability. Teachers can deliberately promote this success by providing their students with regular opportunities to solve word problems and communicate their understanding in a structured way. In Part Two of this book, we offer a recommended problem-solving sequence to support the development of problem-solving skills in primary-age students across the grade span. Please refer to Part Two (Chapters 6 through 8) for grade-specific sequences to introduce and develop students' problem-solving skills in kindergarten, grade 1, and grade 2.

It is essential that students experience initial and continuing success with problem solving if they are to develop confidence in their mathematical reasoning ability.

Differentiation

The entire problem-solving process described in this chapter is deliberately designed to support all students of different levels of skill and understanding; thus, this *is* differentiated instruction. However, in addition to the specific strategies suggested in Chapter 1 (many of which also apply to problem solving and are repeated in this section), we offer a few additional guidelines for meeting the learning needs of students at various levels of problem-solving ability.

Select problems that directly match current classroom instruction.

Begin the process with easier problems and fewer steps, so that students experience immediate success and develop a positive attitude toward the process.

Select problems that students can solve in various ways.

Select problems appropriate to students' instructional level and that can be extended or enriched for more able learners.

Have students add the word *because* after each step they write to extend their thinking and support their reasoning.

Teach and apply the problem-solving strategies to a variety of classroom applications and situations.

Provide vocabulary instruction and related support for all students; increase that support for English-language learners.

Post key mathematical vocabulary on a Math Word Wall.

Encourage the use of manipulatives and graphic representations.

Encourage dialogue that emphasizes sense-making, particularly between students who understand the process and those who do not.

Find times during the day to offer one-on-one assistance to struggling students.

Formally Assessing Problem Solving

The first few Problem-Solving Tasks are done mainly to give students the experience of solving problems and becoming familiar with the format for communicating their process and understanding. Teachers review students' initial work only to determine if they have followed directions and completed the process correctly. However, when students have successfully finished one or more Data Sheets and write-ups with their classmates, and when they are able to complete a Problem-Solving Task independently, it is time to involve them in the assessment of their work. Assessment of problem solving begins with the design of a problem-solving rubric. In the following subsections, we describe in detail the steps we follow when involving students in both the design and use of a problem-solving rubric.

Creating a Problem-Solving Rubric

A *rubric* or *scoring guide* (these terms are used synonymously) is a set of performance criteria that enables both teachers and students to know the level or degree of proficiency reached on a particular piece of student work. We believe that all rubrics should use clearly understood, specific language descriptors upon which everyone (students, teachers, parents, and leaders) can agree, and that teachers should create rubrics in collaboration *with* students so that the rubrics will be truly understood *by* students. Many district and state assessments now include rubrics for evaluation of math tasks, but the criteria in them are highly subjective, such as in the example in Figure 2.3.

Note the subjective terminology underlined in the rubric in Figure 2.3. Teachers who attempted to score student papers using this rubric might find it challenging to agree with each other as to exactly what the underlined terms, such as "full" or "substantially," "in large part," or "partial but limited," actually mean. If reaching agreement proves challenging for professional educators, how much more difficult will it be for students to understand these terms?

The teacher-guided, student-generated rubric for mathematical problem solving is a special type of rubric. It must describe the essential criteria for acceptable performance in *specific, observable,* and *measurable* terms. It must produce fair and reliable evaluation of student write-ups. It must also be usable week after week—a generalized, yet still specific math problem-solving scoring guide with language descriptors that everyone understands.

Because it requires a sizeable block of instructional time to involve students in designing and revising assessment criteria, it is impractical to create a task-specific scoring guide for each

GENERALIZED MATH RUBRIC

4

- ❏ <u>Fully</u> accomplishes the purpose of the task
- ❏ Shows <u>full</u> grasp and use of the central mathematical idea
- ❏ Recorded work communicates thinking clearly, using some combination of written, symbolic, or visual means
_____   ____

3

- ❏ <u>Substantially</u> accomplishes the purpose of the task
- ❏ Shows <u>full</u> grasp and use of the central mathematical idea
- ❏ Recorded work <u>in large part</u> communicates thinking

2

- ❏ <u>Partially</u> accomplishes the purpose of the task
- ❏ Shows <u>partial but limited</u> grasp and use of the central mathematical idea
- ❏ Recorded work may be incomplete, misdirected, or not <u>clearly</u> presented

1

- ❏ <u>Little</u> or no progress toward accomplishing the purpose of the task
- ❏ Shows <u>little</u> or no grasp of the central mathematical idea
- ❏ Recorded work is barely (if at all) comprehensible

_____   _____

Problem-Solving Task. In addition, teachers run the risk of "over-rubricizing"—a term we coined to mean involving students in the creation of too many rubrics and thus negating their enthusiasm for designing assessment criteria. Therefore, the problem-solving rubric must be thoughtfully crafted *once,* with an initial investment of time, so that it can be used throughout the rest of the year to evaluate student understanding on *every* Problem-Solving Task assigned.

How to Design the Problem-Solving Rubric

This is the sequence we follow with students each school year when it is time to begin evaluating problem-solving write-ups with a scoring guide.

1. *Decide on your performance levels.* Although Figure 2.4 shows an example of a four-level, primary-grade problem-solving rubric, we recommend using only three performance levels in kindergarten and grade 1. Begin transitioning to a four-level rubric in grade 2. When students are included in designing scoring guide criteria, the fewer performance levels there are, the better. Students can suggest content and quality descriptors more easily when there are only three levels. However, all primary-grade teachers should decide if and when four levels are developmentally appropriate for their students.

   For primary grades, problem-solving rubrics typically use a 3, 2, 1 number scale, but these performance levels can also be designated with three different colors (green, yellow, red), or three different symbols (star, happy face, or straight face), and so on. We recommend using whatever symbols students choose or are used to.

2. *Choose a format.* Teachers select either a holistic or an analytic format. *Analytic* rubrics represent all the criteria for each performance level in a chart format. Each of the problem-solving components (i.e., Data Sheet, math process, math vocabulary, write-up guide directions, and so on) is represented by specific criteria for *each level* of the rubric. The benefit of an analytic rubric is that it provides very specific diagnostic information for teachers—where students are scoring well and in which areas they need to improve. *Holistic* rubrics simply list all the

criteria for a particular level beneath that level label. Holistic rubrics are often easier for students to use because they appear less complex. We recommend using a holistic format for primary-age students.

3. *Consider the problem-solving elements.* Teachers next consider the following list of problem-solving elements before they begin creating the rubric with their students. As you consider each of these elements, decide where you would place each one in the performance levels you have selected, and how you would describe it for that level. This is an excellent activity to do in grade-level teams before each teacher leads his or her class through the creation of a problem-solving rubric with student input.

   - Right answer
   - Wrong answer, right process
   - Clarity of written explanation
   - Mathematical reasoning
   - Proof or verification of answer
   - Simple calculation errors
   - Inclusion of appropriate math vocabulary
   - Following write-up guide directions

4. *Refer to the Problem-Solving Task Write-Up Guide and practice problems to create rubric criteria.* When students and teachers first begin authoring the rubric, they look at the Problem-Solving Task Write-Up Guide and the practice problems displayed around the room to help them think of criteria to include. The Problem-Solving Guide focuses student attention on the important need to match the rubric to the write-up directions. The posters students created provide powerful examples of mathematical

It is important to remember that the criteria included in the problem-solving rubric should emphasize the mathematics students are to communicate in their written work.

reasoning, the use of math vocabulary, the process the students went through to arrive at the solution, and to what degree the written work communicated mathematical understanding. These examples help students think about both quantity and quality criteria to include in the rubric. It is important to remember that the criteria included in the problem-solving rubric should emphasize the *mathematics* students are to communicate in their written work.

5. *Start with "Proficient."* Student problem-solving work that is to be formally assessed should provide evidence of proficiency. For this reason, most teachers and students write the criteria for the "Proficient" level of the rubric first. However, before they can do this effectively, they need to discuss what *proficient* means. Write down suggested synonyms or phrases that convey what proficiency means. Come to an agreement and then write the *specific, observable, measurable criteria* that demonstrate problem-solving proficiency in the appropriate section of the problem-solving rubric.

6. *Next, write the "Exemplary" criteria.* Refer to the criteria for proficiency and then decide what an exemplary problem-solving Data Sheet and write-up should look like. Write specific, observable, measurable criteria *in relation to the "Proficient" criteria.* This level of the scoring guide should provide students with challenging criteria that will enable them to go above and beyond the expectations for proficiency and demonstrate advanced work.

7. *Next, write the "Progressing" and "Beginning" criteria.* We have streamlined and simplified the problem-solving rubric for these two remaining levels (when using four performance

levels) to keep the focus on proficiency and above. If students understand that the goal is proficiency and higher, as defined by the rubric criteria, it makes sense to describe the progressing and beginning levels in relation to proficiency. When students know that they can revise their work to meet any unmet criteria in the "Proficient" category, it becomes much easier for them to evaluate performance in relation to that designated goal.

Figure 2.4 shows a problem-solving rubric that primary teachers and students can use as a guide to design their own. Once the problem-solving rubric is finalized, it can be used to evaluate every Problem-Solving Task, regardless of the particular math strand or standard in focus. *Note:* Second-grade teachers who may have been using a three-level rubric should decide when to transition to a four-level rubric; this transition is needed to familiarize students with the additional performance level that third-grade teachers are sure to use the following year.

Using the Rubric to Assess

Using a simple problem-solving rubric at the K–2 level provides students with specific feedback on their performance. Teaching primary students to self-assess is an important part of a student-centered assessment process. If students help write the rubric, and then use the rubric to self-assess, they make a very real connection between the rubric and the problem-solving work they have completed. For interested readers, our book, *Student Generated Rubrics: An Assessment Model to Help All Students Succeed* (Ainsworth & Christinson, 1998) fully describes the procedure for involving students (from as early as kindergarten)

Figure 2.4	Sample Problem-Solving Scoring Guide (Primary Grades)

Name_____Title of Problem _____

PROBLEM-SOLVING SCORING GUIDE: PRIMARY

Exemplary:

❑ All "Proficient" criteria *plus*:

❑ Written work explains, step by step, the process used to solve the problem

Proficient:

❑ Correct answer

❑ Solves problem on Data Sheet with words, pictures, and/or numbers

❑ Includes number sentence that matches problem

❑ Follows all Problem-Solving Guide directions to complete write-up

Progressing:

❑ Meets 3 of the "Proficient" criteria

Beginning:

❑ Meets fewer than 3 of the "Proficient" criteria

❑ Task to be repeated after remediation

Self-Evaluation _____

I think my score is a_____because _____

Teacher's Evaluation_____because _____

Note: Proficiency must address the *mathematics*.

Students have ongoing opportunities to reflect upon and revise their work with feedback using the scoring guide.

in designing scoring guides and then teaching them how to self-assess their written work.

At the kindergarten level, students use a rubric to receive feedback about following directions and showing a graphic representation (words, pictures, and/or numbers) of their solution on a Data Sheet.

In first grade, students use a rubric to obtain feedback about following directions, showing a graphic representation, and including a simple written expression of their process steps.

Second-graders transition to using a rubric to receive feedback about their independent performance in problem solving.

We recommend giving students more than one opportunity to demonstrate proficiency on a Problem-Solving Task. The scoring guide is a tool for helping students understand and reach proficiency. We all know that, for many students, proficiency does not occur the first time around. Teachers need to decide for themselves to what extent students can use the scoring-guide feedback to revise their work before moving on to a new task.

The best way to explain quality is by showing examples of it. It is important to provide students with exemplars or models of both proficient and exemplary work. This is an essential part of helping students make the connection between *written* descriptions of quality and proficiency and *visible demonstrations* of quality and proficiency specific to the problem-solving write-up requirements.

Benefits of the Problem-Solving and Rubric Assessment Process

Primary teachers who guide students through this problem-solving process and show them how to use the rubric to self-assess will see many benefits. Students who consistently and regularly engage in structured problem-solving activities will find themselves better prepared to reason mathematically and to think logically as they get older. They will be able to apply their problem-solving skills successfully, not only in the math classroom and on district and state assessments, but also in the authentic math situations they will encounter throughout life.

Reader's Assignment

Reader's Assignment

Begin designing your problem-solving component based on the information presented in this chapter.

First, select a problem according to the guiding questions for selecting worthwhile problems. Solve that problem as recommended and write up your process using the write-up guide template. Finally, design the first draft of a problem-solving rubric to assess your own students' problem solving.

Refer to the sample Problem-Solving Task Write-Up Guide template in the "Reproducibles" section at the end of this book and the grade-specific problem-solving information presented in Chapters 6,7, and 8. Refer also to Chapter 9 for answers to frequently asked questions regarding step 2, Problem Solving.

Step 3: Conceptual Understanding

Essential Questions

What is conceptual understanding? Why is it important in mathematics?

How is conceptual understanding different from procedural understanding?

Definitions

Consider these two definitions from mathematics researcher and author, John Van De Walle (2004, p. 27), and then determine how they match or extend your own.

> *Conceptual knowledge of mathematics consists of logical relationships constructed internally and existing in the mind as a network of ideas .... By its very nature, conceptual knowledge is knowledge that is understood.*

> *Procedural knowledge of mathematics is knowledge of the rules and the procedures that one uses in carrying out routine mathematical tasks and also the symbolism that is used to represent mathematics.*

Rationale

Educators deserve to know the "why" of a new process before they are expected to engage in the "how" of it. The following four passages thoughtfully address persuasive reasons for designing and teaching a conceptual unit of mathematics:

> If we want students to know what mathematics is, as a subject, they must understand it. Knowing mathematics, really knowing it, means understanding it. When we memorize rules for moving symbols around on a paper we may be learning something, but we are not learning mathematics.

> When we memorize names and dates we are not learning history; when we memorize titles of books and authors we are not learning literature. Knowing a subject means getting inside it and seeing how things work, how things are related to each other, and why they work like they do (Hiebert, 1997, p. 2).

> Investigations have consistently shown that an emphasis on teaching for meaning has positive effects on student learning, including better initial learning, greater retention, and increased likelihood that the ideas will be used in new situations. These results have also been found in studies conducted in high-poverty areas (Cawelti, 1999, p. 120).

> If students don't understand the concepts, then it's likely that they're going to forget, and the teachers are going to have to go back and review and review (Hiebert, 2003, p. 24).

The Conceptual Understanding Unit of Study

Designing a conceptual unit of mathematical study is an effective way for teachers to counteract the conventional practice of relying on the math textbook to dictate what to teach and how to assess learning. Developing a conceptual unit enables teachers to examinethe standards and decide what is truly essential for student success (often referred to as *Power Standards*—described in Chapter 5) and then use those identified essentials to focus their day-to-dayplanning of instruction, learning activities, and assessment. A conceptual approach to learning mathematics helps students develop depth of mathematical understanding by connecting meaning to procedures.

Without the understanding that comes from meaning-based instruction, students do not retain information. An example of this is the topic of subtraction. Some students do not connect the underlying mathematical concepts that: (1) subtraction withregrouping is based on the place-value system; (2) numbers can be regrouped to equal the same value; and (3) addition andsubtraction are inverse operations. These students will likely struggle to memorize and retain the *procedure* of subtractioninto the upper elementary grades.

Developing students' conceptual understanding is at the heart of effective mathematics instruction. Step 3 of a balanced mathprogram is designed to help teachers, whether working alone or collaboratively, prepare a conceptual unit aimed at deepeningstudent understanding of that unit's central mathematical focus.

A conceptual approach to learning mathematics helps students develop depth of mathematical understanding by connecting meaning to procedures.

Designing a Conceptual Unit

The conceptual understanding step is the portion of the math hour during which students engage in a lesson or activity as part of a focused mathematics unit of study that lasts from two to four weeks. The Conceptual Understanding Unit lesson and related learning activities take place at the conclusion of Math Review and Mental Math, and require approximately 35 minutes.

Here is an overview of the 20-step sequence we follow when designing, teaching, and assessing a conceptual unit. This sequence and the particular terms used in it are described in detail in later sections.

1. *Establish the central mathematical focus for the unit*—a particular topic that students need to learn in depth. For example, a unit focus could be patterns, or it might be addition, subtraction with regrouping, money, and so on.

2. *Locate the grade-specific math standards* addressing that particular topic.

3. *"Unwrap" those identified standards* to determine the *concepts* (what students need to know) and the *skills* (what students need to be able to do).

4. *Determine the essential mathematical concepts* using the knowledge package process (described later in this chapter).

5. *Decide on the Big Ideas* (the important understandings students are to discover *on their own* by the end of the unit).

6. *Write the Essential Questions* that will focus both instruction and assessment and lead students to discover the Big Ideas.

Designing a Conceptual Unit

7. *Design an end-of-unit post-assessment* closely aligned to the "unwrapped" concepts, skills, and Big Ideas.

8. *Create a rubric or scoring guide* to evaluate the post-assessment.

9. *Design a pre-assessment* aligned to the end-of-unit post-assessment and an accompanying scoring guide.

10. *Plan the instructional lessons* and activities for the unit, guided by the Essential Questions.

11. *Share the Essential Questions* for the unit with students and post the questions visibly in the classroom.

12. *Administer the pre-assessment* to students.

13. *Score the pre-assessments* using the accompanying scoring guide and analyze the results to differentiate instruction.

14. *Begin teaching the unit* according to the planned instructional lessons and activities.

15. *Assess student understanding* informally throughout the unit, using assessment results to make appropriate changes in instruction.

16. *Share with students* the post-assessment scoring guide and then administer the assessment.

17. *Peer-, self-, and teacher-assess* the completed post-assessment using the accompanying scoring guide.

18. *Ask students to write a self-reflection* about their learning in relation to their assessment results.

19. *Create individual student folders* for the collection of important student work products, including formative assessments and the end-of-unit post-assessment.

20. *Spend a few moments* engaged in your own self-reflection.

Writing curriculum and designing units of study is time-intensive work, best accomplished in collaboration with one or more grade-level colleagues.

The Value of Planning a Unit Collaboratively

Writing curriculum and designing units of study is time-intensive work, best accomplished in collaboration with one or more grade-level colleagues. Whether done before the start of a new school year, or completed during the year as needed, it takes time to think deeply about the essential mathematical understandings we want students to develop. Nevertheless, this investment of time yields one of the classroom teacher's best returns: planned instruction and assessment that lead to greater student understanding.

In many respects, teaching is still an isolated profession. Teachers rarely receive the valuable opportunity to collaborate with colleagues. Whatever instructional planning they do is usually done alone and on their own time—even though we know the power of two or more teachers gathered together to plan cooperatively. We see this collaboration as a critical need for schools and districts that are serious about implementing instructional change.

Teachers belong at the center of all instructional decisions. When encouraged to use their experience and knowledge of subject matter to develop curricular focus, they create powerful learning experiences for students.

Here, then, are the details of the 20 steps to designing, teaching, and assessing a conceptual unit of understanding in mathematics. A conceptual unit design template that can be duplicated for instructional use appears in the "Reproducibles" section at the end of this book.

1. *Establish the central mathematical focus for the unit — a particular topic that students need to learn in depth.*
   Working with your grade-level colleague(s), identify a

particular concept that students typically struggle with, one that requires more time and hands-on learning activities than usual for students to really understand it. For primary-grade students, such topics might include number sense, estimation, subtraction, subtraction with regrouping, money, time, and elapsed time, to name but a few. This identified topic will become the focus of the unit you will design and teach conceptually.

2. *Locate the grade-specific math standards addressing that particular topic.* Refer to the district or state math standards for your grade level and find the specific standards or indicators that match the mathematical focus you have selected for your unit.

3. *"Unwrap" those identified standards to determine the concepts (what students need to know) and the skills (what students need to be able to do).* To "unwrap" standards, first read carefully the wording of each standard you have identified. Underline the important *concepts* (nouns or noun phrases) and circle the *skills* (verbs) related to those concepts. Then, represent those concepts and skills on a graphic organizer of choice (a bulleted list, outline, or concept map). Here is an example of an "unwrapped" math standard for the conceptual unit topic of estimation. Note that the skill "applies" has been capitalized rather than circled:

> **Estimation standard:** The student APPLIES numerical estimation with whole numbers up to 999, simple fractions, and money.
>
> Concepts:
>> Estimation
>> - Numerical estimation
>> - Whole numbers to 999

- Simple fractions
- Money

Skills:

- APPLIES (estimation with whole numbers, fractions, money)

Source: Ainsworth, 2003a.

4. *Determine the essential mathematical concepts using the knowledge package process.* The knowledge package method, described near the end of this chapter, is another way in which teachers can find the essential mathematics within a standard. Please refer to the section entitled "The Knowledge Package Process" for details.

5. *Decide on the Big Ideas (the important understandings students are to discover on their own by the end of the unit).* In planning a conceptual unit together, grade-level colleagues ask, "What two or three essential mathematical understandings [Big Ideas] do we want the students to discover *on their own* by the time they complete this unit of study?" This question and the ensuing discussion to determine the essential focus of the unit are extremely important. They help the participating teachers clarify, in advance of instruction, the main ideas students need to understand or important conclusions students need to draw about the standard(s) the teachers are preparing to teach. Here are two suggested Big Ideas relating to the "unwrapped" concepts and skills in the preceding estimation-standard example:

> *Estimation comes close to an exact number.*
>
> *Whether you need to estimate or find the exact answer depends on the particular situation.*

6. *Write the Essential Questions that will focus both instruction and assessment and lead students to discover the Big Ideas.*

Teachers next write Essential Questions to share with students at the beginning of the unit, to interest them in the topic. These guiding questions—matched to the Big Ideas—forecast the learning goals for the unit of study. Their purpose is to help students make insightful connections about the "unwrapped" math concepts and skills they are learning. Students will eventually respond to these Essential Questions with the Big Ideas stated in their own words.

However, the Essential Questions for a conceptual unit do much more than inform students about what they are going to learn. They serve as an *instructional filter* for teachers to use when deciding which lessons and activities are necessary to develop student understanding of the unit's key focus. They enable teachers to determine if the math textbook program is sufficient to teach the particular "unwrapped" concepts and skills, or whether teachers need to search out supplemental materials that are more closely matched to their instructional needs. If other resources do indeed have to be explored, teachers again apply the filter of the Essential Questions to select the most appropriate instructional materials. In this way, the teacher is making these important decisions rather than relying on the textbook to do so.

Here is a sample pair of Essential Questions for the estimation standard:

What is estimation?
(Estimation comes close to an exact number.)

When and how do we use it?
(Whether you need to estimate or find the exact answer depends on the particular situation.)

Note the corresponding Big Ideas in parentheses. The first Big Idea is a desired student response to the first Essential Question: the student should be able to provide a definition of *estimation*. The second Essential Question and corresponding Big Idea response represent a higher level of thinking; that is, students must make a broader connection and demonstrate their understanding of the concept of estimation in an applied way.

7. *Design an end-of-unit post-assessment closely aligned to the "unwrapped" concepts, skills, and Big Ideas.* As soon as the "unwrapped" concepts, skills, and Big Ideas have been determined, teachers next design a suitable *post-assessment* to administer at the end of the unit. A suitable post-assessment meets two essential criteria. First, it directly aligns with the "unwrapped" concepts, skills, Big Ideas, and Essential Questions that were used to establish the foundation for the unit. Second, it provides students with the opportunity to demonstrate their full range of understanding of the "unwrapped" concepts and skills and allows them to respond to the Essential Questions with Big-Idea responses stated in their own words.

To meet these two requirements, teachers often design a performance-based assessment *and* a more traditional type of math assessment. With more than one type of assessment, students have the opportunity to demonstrate their understanding in multiple ways. The first assessment type—usually a Problem-Solving Task, as described in Chapter 2—allows students to show to what extent they can apply the math concepts and skills they learned during the unit to a problem-solving situation. Alternatively, teachers may simply ask students to say or write their Big-Idea responses to the Essential Questions. The second type—a more traditional assessment—requires students to solve computation problems matched to the focus of the unit. Teachers review available assessment resources (the math series in use, supplemental materials, and so on) to select assessment items that match their purpose. If they cannot find an appropriate assessment in published materials, they simply create their own.

The end-of-unit post-assessment does not replace the informal assessments *for* learning that teachers routinely conduct on a daily basis. Teachers use the results of ongoing informal assessments to differentiate instruction. This includes providing struggling students with additional assistance or intervention and advanced students with enrichment or acceleration *before* they take the end-of-unit post-assessment. An example of a primary-grade assessment that contains both traditional items and a performance-based task is provided later in this chapter.

8. *Create a rubric or scoring guide to evaluate the post-assessment.* For the traditional assessment, the participating teachers can simply score the student papers as they are accustomed to doing. However, they will, more than likely, need a rubric or scoring guide to evaluate the performance-based portion of the assessment. Establishing clear-cut criteria *in advance* will help students better understand the assessment directions and will enable them to set personal goals for their learning.

To design a scoring guide with either three or four performance levels, refer back to the assessment itself. Identify the specific

> *Establishing clear-cut criteria* in advance *will help students better understand the assessment directions and will enable them to set personal goals for their learning.*

elements the students are to include in their written work. Then, write *specific* descriptors that will let students know exactly what they have to do to demonstrate proficiency on the assessment. After that, write the specific descriptors for the other performance levels. The rubric levels can be labeled with letters, numbers, words, or symbols. Lower primary grades often use a star, happy face, and straight face, or different colors. Use whatever labels work best for student understanding. (For additional guidelines, please refer again to the section on writing a math rubric with students in Chapter 2.)

9. *Design a pre-assessment aligned to the end-of-unit post-assessment and an accompanying scoring guide.* Before beginning any instructional planning for the conceptual unit, teachers design a pre-assessment matched to the format and items of the post-assessment. Usually they can use the same rubric that they developed for the post-assessment to evaluate the pre-assessment student papers (as long as the assessments are the same or similar).

10. *Plan the instructional lessons and activities for the unit, guided by the Essential Questions.* With grade-level colleagues, teachers now review their math series and any supplemental materials through the lens of their Essential Questions and decide on the specific instructional activities that will advance student understanding of the unit focus. This filtering process promotes the alignment of curriculum, instruction, and assessment. All lessons and activities presented during the course of the unit should prepare students for success on the post-assessment(s).

If a particular lesson or activity matches the Essential Questions, great! If it does not align, determine whether it can be modified so that it does. If it cannot be modified, continue searching resources for lessons or activities that can be.

11. *Share the Essential Questions for the unit with students and post the questions visibly in the classroom.* To set the stage for the upcoming unit, the teacher displays the Essential Questions in the classroom and lets students know that by the end of the unit, they will need to be able to respond to each of those questions. The teacher then asks students to give initial responses to the questions. This enables students to begin thinking about the topic of the unit and gives the teacher insights as to what students may already know about this subject.

12. *Administer the pre-assessment to students.* Teachers next let students know that they need students to complete a pre-assessment, to help the teachers plan their instruction. Tell students that the pre-assessment will be very similar to what they will see on the post-assessment at the end of the unit. Ask students to do their best, but remind them not to worry if they do not know the answers, because they have not yet been taught this information. Then, administer the pre-assessment to the students.

13. *Score the pre-assessments using the accompanying scoring guide and analyze the results to differentiate instruction.* The chief benefit of giving a pre-assessment is that it enables teachers to find out, before any instruction takes place, which students are already proficient and need enrichment or acceleration, which students are almost proficient, and which

students are far from proficient and will likely need intervention. These assessment results will greatly assist teachers in differentiating instruction for all their students as part of their unit planning.

14. *Begin teaching the unit according to the planned instructional lessons and activities.* We believe that students need the opportunity to wrestle with mathematical ideas to construct personal meaning. Here, *depth of student understanding* is the teacher's goal. To achieve this, present the selected activities and lessons as often as possible in a hands-on manner to help students build their own understanding of the "unwrapped" concepts and skills. Remember to incorporate into Math Review and Mental Math the computational skills that relate to the conceptual understanding of the topic the students are studying.

    Students complete the conceptual lessons and activities individually, in pairs, cooperatively in teams, and/or together as a class. Often we evaluate these formative activities only for completion and demonstration of students' current level of understanding, using this feedback to modify and improve our instruction.

15. *Assess student understanding informally throughout the unit, using assessment results to make appropriate changes in instruction.* More and more, teachers are realizing the value of conducting informal assessments *for* learning. These assessments are formative, shorter in length and duration than more formal evaluations, and provide timely feedback to both students and teacher. Students use the results from such ongoing assessments to reflect on their performance, measure

their progress toward attainment of their personal learning goals, and make a plan for improvement. Teachers use the results from these "check-in" assessments to monitor and adjust instruction to meet the varying needs of all students.

16. *Share with students the post-assessment scoring guide and then administer the assessment.* When all instruction and learning activities for the conceptual unit have been completed, inform the students that it is time for the end-of-unit assessment. Distribute the scoring guide that will be used to evaluate the student responses on the performance portion of the assessment, explain the criteria, and encourage students to refer to the scoring guide for guidance as they complete their post-assessments.

17. *Peer-, self-, and teacher-assess the completed post-assessment using the accompanying scoring guide.* Kindergarten and first-grade students should be encouraged to self-assess their performance on the post-assessment to help them decide if they followed directions. Second-grade students may be able to assess the work of their peers. After the children self- and peer-assess their work, teachers complete the final evaluation of students' end-of-unit assessments.

As described in step 2, teaching students how to assess their own work and the work of their peers (when developmentally appropriate) increases individual student understanding of the evaluation process. By seeing a variety of work samples, primary-grade students come to understand that there are different levels of work quality. Presenting students with various models of proficient and exemplary work helps them to produce that level of quality themselves.

Presenting students with various models of proficient and exemplary work helps them to produce that level of quality themselves.

18. *Ask students to write a self-reflection about their learning in relation to their assessment results.* After returning the evaluated post-assessments to students, ask students to respond to three self-reflection questions:

    - *What did I learn well during this unit?*
    - *What do I still need to work on?*
    - *What is my plan to improve?*

    These questions help students to determine to what degree they learned the concepts, skills, and Big Ideas of the unit and to identify specific areas in which they need to improve. It is important to ask students to write a sentence or two (kindergarten students do this orally) setting out their specific plan for improvement during the next math unit, so that they take ownership of their own learning process.

19. *Create individual student folders for the collection of important student work products, including formative assessments and the end-of-unit post-assessment.* This is an organizational and management step that can occur whenever teachers wish. A folder or other organized collection of key student work products and assessments is a practical way to keep track of all completed unit papers. Teachers do this by placing the selected student papers in construction-paper folders or index file folders marked with individual student names. These folders may also include any Problem-Solving Task write-ups related to the conceptual unit focus.

    Students can take part in this process by labeling the cover of the folder with their names, title of the math unit, and any other identifying information required. On the inside cover, list the four criteria that the teacher will use to grade the folder:

- Neat
- Complete
- On time
- Organized

A student's completed unit folder can be sent home for parent review and comments before the teacher places it into the mathematics portfolio. The portfolio is an ongoing collection of the year's math conceptual unit folders that is reviewed during parent conferences and at other times during the school year. Teachers may also copy and forward representative samples of student learning to the next year's math teacher. The unit folders in the portfolio are given to the student at the end of the academic year.

20. *Spend a few moments engaged in your own self-reflection.*
With the conceptual unit now completed, teachers can use the following questions to reflect on the success of the unit:

- *What went well in the design and implementation of this unit? What did not?*

- *What insights into student learning did the pre- and post-assessments yield?*

- *What changes or improvements do I want to make when I teach this unit the next time?*

- *What changes or improvements do I want to make when designing my next unit?*

> *The portfolio is an ongoing collection of the year's math conceptual unit folders that is reviewed during parent conferences and at other times during the school year.*

Primary Example of Conceptual Unit Planning

Many states now include a specific standard for problem solving and provide grade-specific learning expectations (*indicators*) for meeting that standard. Because problem solving is a widely recognized area of need in terms of student performance on state mathematics assessments, we selected this topic to illustrate the foundational design of a primary-grade conceptual unit.

Here are the key components of a grade 1 Conceptual Understanding Unit to address the topic of problem solving:

The "unwrapped" standards, with accompanying Big Ideas and Essential Questions

The performance-based, end-of-unit post-assessment

The matching rubric or scoring guide to evaluate student proficiency

Once this foundation for the unit is established, grade 1 teachers can use it as a guide to select appropriate lessons and hands-on learning activities from their particular textbook series and supplemental instructional materials. A planning template for designing a complete conceptual unit appears in the "Reproducibles" section at the end of this book. Figure 3.1 shows an example of a completed conceptual unit design. In addition, readers will find a conceptual unit appropriate for kindergarten, grade 1, and grade 2 students in Chapters 6, 7, and 8, respectively. Chapter 9 sets out a weekly teaching schedule that includes a conceptual unit and the other components of our balanced math program model.

Primary Example of Conceptual Unit Planning

Figure 3.1	Sample Completed Conceptual Unit Design

Grade: 1

Conceptual Unit Focus:
Problem Solving

Standards and Indicators Matched to Unit Focus:
[Here teachers list and "unwrap" the full text of the relevant standard and indicators from individual district or state documents for the selected topic.]

"Unwrapped" Concepts:

Need to Know about Problem Solving

Set Up Problems:
❏ Problem solving
❏ Model

Solve Problems and Reason:
❏ Procedures and results
❏ Connections

Skills: Be Able to Do:
❏ Choose (approach, materials, and strategies)
❏ Use (tools)
❏ Explain (reasoning)
❏ Justify (procedures)
❏ Make (calculations)
❏ Check (validity)
❏ Understand and use (connections)

Topics or Context [resources teachers will use to teach the concepts and skills]:
❏ Mathematics textbook
❏ Everyday Counts

❏ Mountain Math
❏ TLC (Teaching and Learning with Computers) stations

Big Ideas:

1. A story problem tells a story using words and numbers.
2. To solve a story problem, you have to start with what you know and figure out what you don't know.
3. A number sentence helps you find the answer to the problem.

Essential Questions:

1. What is a story problem, and how do you solve it?
2. What is a number sentence? Why do we use it?

End-of-Unit Performance-Based Assessment: "Fish Tank Problem"

At the fish store there are several fish swimming in 2 large tanks.

Some fish have 5 spots.

Some fish have 3 spots.

Some fish have 2 spots.

You look at each tank and see 18 spots in each tank, but the two tanks have different fish. Use pictures and numbers to show how the fish could look in each tank.

Write a number sentence for your problem.

Now use words and numbers to explain your answer.

Scoring Guide:

Exemplary:

❏ All "Proficient" criteria met *plus*:
❏ Describes strategy used to solve problem
❏ Includes more than one number sentence to show a different way to solve

Proficient:

❏ Pictures and numbers correctly show how fish look in each tank
❏ Correct number sentence
❏ Correct use of words and numbers to explain answer

Progressing:

❏ Meets 2 of the "Proficient" criteria

Beginning:

❏ Meets fewer than 2 of the "Proficient" criteria
❏ Assessment task to be repeated after remediation

Self-Evaluation

_____

Teacher's Evaluation

_____

_____

Source: K–7 Math Performance Task Binder. Special thanks to the San Diego County Office of Education and the K–2 Performance Assessment Team for permission to reprint this assessment.

Other Considerations

There are other useful strategies to consider when designing a Conceptual Understanding Unit to best meet the learning needs of all primary-grade students. In the following section, we present a knowledge package idea that can be used along with the "unwrapping" process to pinpoint the particular concepts students need to learn in depth for a particular topic. To conclude this chapter, we provide a powerful process for vocabulary development, applicable not only to mathematics but also to all other content areas.

The Knowledge Package Process

The knowledge package process was listed earlier as the fourth step of the conceptual unit design sequence. It provides teachers with another effective method for determining the essential mathematical focus of a conceptual unit. Because the knowledge package process is worthy of consideration in and of itself, we include a separate description of it here.

In her book, *Knowing and Teaching Elementary Mathematics*, Liping Ma described a *knowledge package* as a "group of topics that teachers tend to see around the topic they are teaching" (1999, p. 118). She stated, "You should see a knowledge package when you are teaching a piece of knowledge. You have to know that the knowledge you are teaching is supported by [particular] ideas or procedures" (p. 18). For example, the operation of subtraction with regrouping (which Liping Ma refers to as "decomposition of numbers") is *the application of several ideas* rather than a single idea. "It is a package, rather than a sequence of knowledge" (p. 17).

The Knowledge Package Process

We present the following knowledge package activity in our *Five Easy Steps to a Balanced Math Program* workshops to assist educators in identifying the essential mathematical understanding to be developed during a unit of study. This activity, usually completed by a grade-level team of teachers planning together, helps teachers determine the understandings students must have to be successful with a particular math concept.

Make a *cluster* of the concepts, skills, and procedures that are related to a selected math topic.

Decide which parts of the cluster are *procedural* and which are *conceptual*.

Discuss which parts of the cluster represent the *essential mathematical understandings* necessary for student success.

Use these essential mathematical understandings to help develop *Big Ideas* and *Essential Questions* for the conceptual unit.

For example, consider the topic of subtraction with regrouping. Working together, grade-level teachers create a cluster that shows all the concepts, skills, ideas, and vocabulary that are connected to subtraction with regrouping. Figure 3.2 is an example of this kind of knowledge package cluster.

In the second part of the activity, the grade-level teachers discuss the items in the cluster and decide which ones are most important for students to understand about the topic of subtraction with regrouping. They ask: "What is the key concept? What do students need to understand to be successful with the process of subtraction with regrouping?" Through this discussion, it will become evident that there is really only one essential understanding to grasp about

Figure 3.2   Example of Knowledge Package Cluster

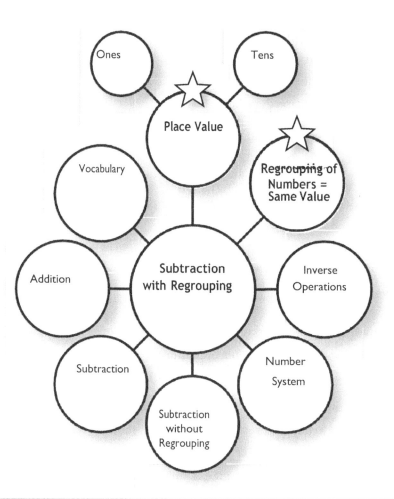

the concept of subtraction with regrouping: a given quantity can be regrouped in a different way without changing its value.

Next, teachers decide which of the items in the cluster are more likely to be taught conceptually and which are more likely to be taught procedurally. Usually they agree that most of the items in the cluster are taught *procedurally*. They admit that subtraction with regrouping is typically taught as a mechanical procedure, whereby students cross out numbers and place values on top of other numbers. After further discussion, the grade-level teachersusually realize that for students to understand subtraction with regrouping, it is absolutely essential that they understand place value in our number system, and that numbers can be regrouped*without changing the value of the number.*

For example, the number 23 (2 tens and 3 ones) can be regrouped into 1 ten and 13 ones. Therefore, students will understand and be successful with regrouping if instruction during the conceptual unit focuses on place value and regrouping of numbers rather than procedures that are done mechanically without studentsunderstanding why.

The main benefit of the knowledge package discussion activityis that it allows teachers to identify the *essential mathematical understandings* (Big Ideas) that they will then emphasize conceptually during a unit of study focused on the chosen topic. We urgeprimary-grade teachers to try to create a knowledge package for a selected topic before planning the instructional lessons and activities for teaching that topic.

The results of student assessment in mathematics are directly affected by student knowledge of mathematical vocabulary.

Differentiation and Vocabulary Development

The results of student assessment in mathematics are directly affected by student knowledge of mathematical vocabulary. In his book, *Building Background Knowledge for Academic Achievement,* Robert Marzano described a six-step process for providing students with direct instruction in vocabulary.

Step 3: Conceptual Understanding

The process involves the teacher describing vocabulary terms; students constructing their own descriptions of terms; students constructing nonlinguistic representations; the teacher providing opportunities for students to review and add to their knowledge of the terms; students interacting about the terms; and students playing games involving vocabulary terms (Marzano, 2004, p. 103).

Jan Christinson developed the following activity that applies Marzano's six-step process to increase student understanding of vocabulary—in this case, mathematical vocabulary. Students record their work in an "academic notebook," a journal in which they write initial definitions for vocabulary words and then continue to refine those definitions over time. (Kindergarten and grade 1 teachers can adapt this activity according to the readiness of their students.)

For example, let us use "circle" as the subject for this activity. The vocabulary words for this subject are *circle, diameter, radius,* and *circumference.* The procedure is as follows:

Step 1   Students individually cluster what they know about a circle. After clustering, each student shares his or her cluster with a partner and adds to his or her own cluster during the sharing.

Step 2   The teacher presents to the class a teacher-made definition of each math word, and then repeats that definition. Students paraphrase the teacher's definition in writing and draw a graphic representation to match. After writing their paraphrased definitions, students discuss them with partners and revise if necessary. They then repeat the process for each of the words presented.

Differentiation and Vocabulary Development

Step 3 Working in small groups of three or four, students create similes or metaphors for the vocabulary words and then share those with the class. Here are two examples:

- A radius is like a spoke on a wheel.
- Circumference is a snake biting its tail.

Step 4 After they complete the metaphor-and-simile activity, students revise their paraphrased definitions in their academic notebooks.

Step 5 While in the same groups, students play a pantomime game. One member of the group is chosen to act out one of the circle words. The other members of the group try to guess the word from the pantomimed visual clues.

Step 6 Without referring to their notes, students create a cluster to show all that they now know about a circle. After doing this, they self-reflect by referring to the notes they took during the earlier steps.

We encourage readers to experiment with this powerful activity to develop student knowledge of mathematical vocabulary.

Step 3: Conceptual Understanding

Reader's Assignment

Locate the conceptual unit planning template in the "Reproducibles" section of this book. Working with your grade-level colleagues, begin designing a math unit based on this conceptual unit model. First, determine your topic; then find the grade-specific standards or indicators that match. "Unwrap" the standards or indicators to find the concepts and skills. Apply the knowledge package process described earlier in this chapter. Decide on your Big Ideas and write your Essential Questions. Then, design an end-of- unit post-assessment directly aligned with your "unwrapped"concepts and skills and with your Big Ideas. Write the scoringguide that you will use to evaluate student performance
on the post-assessment. After that, follow the remaining sequence of steps provided in this chapter, including the math vocabulary development suggestions.

Refer to the sample kindergarten, grade 1, and grade 2 conceptual units in Chapters 6, 7, and 8, respectively. Refer also to Chapter 9 for answers to frequently asked questions about step 3, Conceptual Understanding.

Step 4: Mastery of Math Facts

Essential Questions

How do students learn their math facts? How should *they learn them?*

Do you have an accountability system in place so that students not only learn but also retain their math facts?

Has a timeline been established to determine when students will learn all their math facts?

Rationale

Just as learning to count is a prerequisite skill that very young children need before they can begin exploring and manipulating number concepts, mastery of basic number facts is necessary as students move through the first formal years of schooling. By the time students leave elementary school, they should have these facts firmly committed to memory—yet the majority of middle school teachers report that this is not the case. The fourth step in our balanced math program suggests ways in which elementary-grade teachers can help their students master basic math facts *before* they enter middle school.

Students who do not learn their math facts have great difficulty solving problems accurately and in an appropriate amount of time. Not only does this cause them frustration, but it also weakens their perception of themselves as mathematically powerful students, undermining the self-concept that we as educators are striving so diligently to promote and achieve through our unit planning, our engaging lessons and activities, and our methods of assessment.

Marilyn Burns has this to say with regard to students learning their basic number facts: "Memorization plays an important role in computation. Calculating mentally or with paper and pencil requires having basic number facts committed to memory. However, memorization should follow, not lead, instruction that builds children's understanding. The emphasis of learning in mathematics must always be on thinking, reasoning, and making sense" (1999, p. 408). How, then, do we help students master the necessary skill of being able to fluently and accurately recall their math facts?

Implementing Step 4

Emphasize Patterns

We have found that helping students discover patterns makes it easier and more interesting for them to learn and retain number facts. Therefore, we strive to create a classroom environment that emphasizes patterns, presents number facts in a way that makes sense, and reinforces fact acquisition through regular practice. Read what respected math researcher and author John Van De Walle has to say about teaching students math facts:

Fortunately, we know quite a bit about helping children develop fact mastery, and it has little to do with quantity of drill or drill techniques. Three components or steps to this end can be identified:

1. *Help children develop a strong understanding of the operations and of number relationships.*

2. *Develop efficient strategies for fact retrieval through practice.*

3. *Then provide drill in the use and selection of those strategies once they have been developed*

(Van De Walle, 2004, p. 157).

We recommend presenting lessons that demonstrate the various patterns in our number system. Patterns that will help K–2 students learn math facts and develop improved number sense include:

One more than and two more than a number
(8 +1, 8 + 2, and so on)

Facts with zero (0 + 2, 0 + 3, and so on)

Doubles (2 + 2, 5 + 5, 9 + 9, and so on)

Facts that make five (3 + 2, 2 +3, and so on)

Facts that make ten (7 + 3, 2 + 8, and so on)

Part-part-whole relationships (fact-family groups)

Addition and subtraction as inverse operations

Once students feel comfortable with these patterns and can recall answers accurately, drill and practice using these strategies will help students become increasingly efficient in recalling basic facts. "Adopt this simple rule and stick with it: Do not subject any student to fact drills unless the student has developed an efficient strategy for the facts included in the drill" (Van De Walle, 2004, p. 174).

Determine Grade-Appropriate Facts

To determine *when* children should master their addition and subtraction facts in primary grades, and multiplication and division facts in upper elementary grades, start by referencing district and state mathematics standards and discussing grade-level expectations with colleagues. It is essential to agree upon this at the individual school site. When teachers decide together which

We strive to create a classroom environment that emphasizes patterns, presents number facts in a way that makes sense, and reinforces fact acquisition through regular practice.

facts should be learned in first grade, second grade, and so on, and then communicate these expectations to parents, the cumulative result at the end of elementary school is a body of students who know their facts!

Kindergarten students need lots of beginning practice with number combinations that make 5 and later 10. Typically, first-grade students work with addition facts up through 10, but the state standards may expect students to learn their facts up to and including 20. Teachers usually agree that a developmentally appropriate expectation for second-graders is that they learn addition *and* subtraction facts up to 20. Third-graders continue practicing addition and subtraction facts and begin learning easier multiplication facts (twos, threes, fours, fives, nines, and tens). They discover the relationship between addition and multiplication (repeated addition, such as 3 +3+3 representing three groups of three or 3 x 3= 9). Fourth-graders maintain their fluency with addition and subtraction facts while also working to master the remaining multiplication facts and the corresponding division facts.

We believe that fifth grade is the year when students need to demonstrate that they have mastered the number facts in all four basic operations. Fifth-graders are on the verge of entering middle school mathematics classes, where such prior learning is expected. Therefore, we hold them more rigorously accountable than we do younger children.

Readers will find suggestions for teaching math facts that are appropriate for kindergarten, grade 1, and grade 2 students in Chapters 6, 7, and 8, respectively. Refer also to the "Reproducibles" section at the end of this book, which includes a summary of the patterns we recommend emphasizing in each grade, K–5, along with suggestions for helping students learn their facts both at school and at home.

Inform Parents at Beginning of Year

Parents can play a major role in helping their children practice and learn basic math facts. Parents understand the importance of learning math facts because they once had to learn them, too! Students know that they need to learn their math facts—teachers tell them so every year—yet not all students motivate themselves to do so. Parental support and assistance are therefore essential, and it is up to the teacher to communicate the need for that support and then establish a program of accountability to ensure that each student receives it. Traditional events at the beginning of the school year, such as Back-to-School Night and distribution of the teacher's welcome letter, provide excellent opportunities to inform parents of the specific math facts their children will need to learn that year.

Establish Timeline to Assess Progress

At the beginning of a school year, we allow two or three months of practice before holding students accountable by means of a math facts assessment. After that, we establish a regular assessment schedule as described later in this chapter.

It is important to let parents know how often students will be assessed for fact recall. Our experience has been that with a regular system of accountability (a weekly or biweekly quiz, for example), there is a much greater likelihood that students and parents will make the mastery of facts a priority.

> *At the beginning of a school year, we allow two or three months of practice before holding students accountable by means of a math facts assessment.*

Step 4: Mastery of Math Facts

We also believe in keeping parents informed of theirchildren's progress as the year continues by sending home the results of each math facts assessment.

We also believe in keeping parents informed of their children's progress as the year continues by sending home the results of each math facts assessment. We require students who do not demonstrate mastery on those periodic assessments to do extra practice nightly until mastery is achieved and verified through subsequent reassessment.

Assess What Students Presently Know

When beginning your program to promote mastery of math facts, first assess what students currently know, by using a written or oral quiz. Thereafter, systematically build into the math program regular opportunities for children to practice facts, in as non- threatening a climate as possible. As described later, the Math Review and Mental Math portions of the daily math period provideexcellent practice opportunities for students to do this.

In both primary and upper elementary grades, teachers generally use their own self-made assessments, commercially produced assessments, or both. Whatever the format used, and regardlessof whether that format is used in only one classroom or across several grade levels within a school, our recommendation is tochoose a format that works and use it consistently.

Provide Daily Practice Materials

The key to unlocking student success with math facts, *before* formal testing, is regular, systematic practice, both in school and at home. Here are several suggestions for helping primary-grade students master their number facts with home and in-school practice:

> **Orally practice "one more than" and "two more than" a given number.**

Implementing Step 4

Practice different ways to make a number
(e.g., 1+5 = 6; 2+4 = 6; 3+3 =6).

Practice doubles orally or with flash cards.

Practice with five-frames and ten-frames (see Figure 4.1).

Play board games that involve addition and subtraction.

Play math-facts games on the Internet and utilize computer
software math-facts programs.

Use practice worksheets.

Read literature books that involve counting, adding, and
subtracting in the story line.

A Five-Frame and a Ten-Frame

Figure 4.1

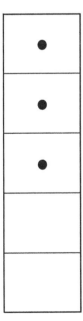 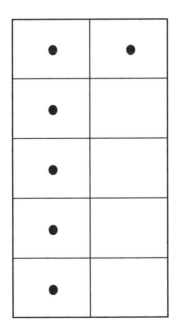

Source: Adapted from Van De Walle, 2004, p. 122.

Math Review and Mental Math

Math Review and Mental Math also provide excellent opportunities for students to practice and learn their math facts, while they solve procedural math problems or mentally calculate a sequence of numbers and operations. Number sense and math facts are reinforced and developed when teachers emphasize "reasonable answer" and the different ways to solve a problem during the processing of Math Review and Mental Math. Students learn to use the facts they know to find the facts they are not sure of. Developing a strong understanding of the number system and its patterns will help students develop confidence in the other areas of mathematics.

A Simple Management System

Regular administration of math facts assessments can be a demanding task, especially if the teacher has to score all the papers, keep track of which students need to be reassessed, and then schedule those assessments (including makeups for absent students). We have used the following system with excellent results.

We set up an expanding file system, using Pendaflex folders or something similar, and label the different folders according to the specific facts for addition and subtraction. We keep the files stocked with copies of the initial assessment, practice papers for homework, and subsequent assessments. Students can be taught how to go to the files and select the particular assessment they need.

Helping Students Handle Time Pressure

Most students like the challenge of writing the sum or difference under an addition or subtraction fact problem. Ask students to perform within a limited time, under time constraints, and that enjoyment remains high for those who love challenges—but it plummets drastically for those who do not. All the rationale in the world about why these assessments should be timed prove ineffective when students are trying their best to perform, but just cannot get those answers on the paper fast enough.

How fast should students be expected to perform accurately on a math-facts assessment? This is an issue to be decided by individual teachers, grade levels, or the entire school. Caring as teachers do about promoting positive self-esteem in the mathematics classroom, it seems counterproductive to apply a time constraint to the administration of an assessment, knowing the effect it will have on certain students. Consider the words of Marilyn Burns on the subject of timed tests:

> Teachers who use timed tests believe that the tests help children learn basic facts. This perspective makes no instructional sense. Children who perform well under time pressure display their skills. Children who have difficulty with skills, or who work more slowly, run the risk of reinforcing wrong practices under pressure. Also, they can become fearful about, and negative toward, their mathematics learning (Burns, 1995, p. 408).

Timed tests are a traditional method of math assessment, but alternate methods should be made available to students who are greatly frustrated by a time constraint. A timed test is an *assessment*; it is not instruction. Timed testing does not teach

Urge students to practice at home with their parents every night and to use word and number associations or other creative ways to remember the facts that are difficult for them.

students math facts. Students learn math facts from good instruction. Primary-grade teachers may decide that it is not developmentally appropriate to give their young students timed math-facts assessments. Nevertheless, a long-standing practice in American education has been to assess student recall of math facts within predetermined time limits. For teachers who decide that they must continue requiring students to complete a certain number of problems within a specified time limit, we offer the following suggestions for doing so.

When It Is Time to Start Assessing

The first week you plan to assess, send home a letter on Monday to inform parents that your math-facts accountability program is beginning. Give each student a copy of the number facts you have selected to quiz. Tell the class that they will use this paper to practice during the coming week. Announce that on Friday you will give them a clean copy of the same paper, or a different sequence of the same problems that they have studied, to be completed without help within so many minutes. Let them know how much time they will have, and allow them to practice once or twice together so that they can experience working within a time limit before taking the actual quiz.

Urge students to practice at home with their parents every night and to use word and number associations or other creative ways to remember the facts that are difficult for them. Remind them of the patterns they have learned. Remind them also that they have practiced these facts in fun ways at school and at home, and that they already know many of these facts. Encourage them to take a practice quiz at home within the predetermined time limit, so that they simulate the assessment conditions. Announce your criteria for proficient performance. Throughout the week, and even before the assessment on Friday, orally review the facts you will be assessing.

Assessment Day

Distribute a copy of the assessment to each student. Direct students to write their names on their papers, turn their papers over, and wait for the "go" signal. Students often enjoy the synchronized swishing sound when the entire class turns over papers at once and begins. Mark time in minutes, writing the elapsed time on the board for anyone who wants to see. We suggest *not* calling out the time remaining, as this seems to put extra stress on many students.

When 30 seconds remain in the allotted time, direct students to stop, hold their pencils in the air, look down at their papers, and determine how many more facts they need to do. Then, announce that 30 seconds remain and encourage students to write as many more answers in the time left as they can. This seems to help focus students and prepare them for the impending "time's up" announcement.

Primary-grade teachers usually collect and score the assessments themselves. When students are able to do so, they can begin scoring their own or their classmates' papers.

Once you begin assessing students on their math facts, continue this procedure weekly or biweekly so that students regard it as an ongoing, regular part of their balanced math program. These assessments will allow students and parents to gauge progress toward the end goal of mastering *all* the grade-level facts they are responsible for learning that year.

Extra Practice Required

As indicated earlier, we always notify parents of students who do not show an acceptable level of proficiency on a particular math-facts assessment; we also provide them with suggested strategies to help their children become successful. Children are reassessed on these same math facts until they demonstrate proficiency.

Differentiation: Strategies for Struggling Students

By following the suggestions in this chapter and in the grade-specific chapters for kindergarten, grade 1, and grade 2, primary-grade students will develop a solid foundation for the mastery of their math facts. However, primary-grade students who continue struggling to learn their grade-appropriate math facts will benefit from a different approach. Part of the problem may simply be due to developmental readiness. More drill is not the answer! Here are a few suggestions that should prove effective:

Help these students find out which facts they know and which facts they do not. Many students who are struggling or who have become overly frustrated think that they do not know any math facts. This is certainly not true, and teachers need to help these students realize this.

Reemphasize patterns within the number system and help students see that math facts are interconnected.

Find out if the student has a strategy of his or her own that he or she uses to find the answer to an unknown fact. Share among students any of these helpful strategies based on patterns that other students are using.

Involve students in daily Mental Math activities to help them develop their number sense.

Provide students with frequent opportunities to experience success. One way to do this is to focus on a few related math facts at a time. When frustrated students experience even a little success, it can begin to change their entire attitude toward math!

Offer alternate methods of assessing math-facts proficiency (use of flash cards, oral responses, individual assessment, and so on).

Summing Up

It *is* possible to help all students achieve mastery of their basic math facts. Teachers who have been the most successful in producing students who can recall math facts follow this proven three-part formula:

1. Teach math facts in the context of patterns, using the strategies provided earlier in this chapter.
2. Provide ongoing practice, both in and out of the classroom.
3. Establish a regular timeline for assessing math facts; then inform parents and enlist their support.

Step 4: Mastery of Math Facts

Reader's Assignment

Plan how you will incorporate the recommendations described in this chapter into your balanced math program.

1. *Determine the grade-appropriate facts you want your students to master.*

2. *Consider how you will teach math facts through patterns.*

3. *Establish a timeline for regular assessment of student progress and then draft your letter to parents.*

4. *Select your math-facts assessment program and gather necessary instructional and practice materials.*

5. *Reflect on the other suggestions included in this chapter to help you implement this component of your balanced math program.*

6. *Refer to Chapters 6, 7, and 8 for specific suggestions when teaching math facts to kindergarten, grade 1, and grade 2 students, respectively. Refer also to Chapter 9 for answers to frequently asked questions about step 4, Mastery of Math Facts.*

Step 5: Common Formative Assessment

CHAPTER 5

Essential Questions

How are you assessing the effectiveness of math instruction within your grade level, school, or district throughout the school year?

How frequently are you collecting student data from math assessments, and how are you using this data to improve student achievement?

Overview

Common formative assessments are assessments collaboratively designed by a grade-level team of teachers and administered to all of the students in that grade level several times throughout the school year. Teachers use the results of common formative assessments to evaluate student understanding of the essential standards they are currently teaching. Because these assessments are formative by design and intent, they provide participating teachers with the timely feedback needed to differentiate instruction and thus better meet the diverse learning needs of their students. In this way, assessment truly informs instruction.

Grade-level teachers often collaboratively score their common formative assessments, analyze the results together, and discuss ways to achieve improvements in student learning on the next common formative assessment. These instruments are typically designed to be used as both a pre- and a post-assessment (to ensure same-assessment to same-assessment comparison). Thus, participating teachers administer their common formative pre- and post-assessments to measure student growth in understanding from the beginning of an instructional unit (of approximately two to four weeks' duration) until its end. If these in-school, common *formative* assessments are also aligned to the large-scale district and state *summative* assessments, the formative assessment results will reveal what students still need to learn to be successful on those external assessments. These internal assessments thus provide valuable diagnostic information in time for teachers to make needed instructional changes.

Rationale

Most educators agree that the usefulness of data from the annual state assessments is limited, because state data offer only a limited view of how a particular child performed on a given day rather than providing a window into student understanding as viewed over time.

The external state assessment is an assessment *of* students' learning that is summative, whereas the internal classroom assessment is an assessment *for* students' learning that is formative (Stiggins, Arter, Chappuis, & Chappuis, 2004). However, both types of assessment are necessary. "Assessment must be seen as an *instructional tool* for use while learning is occurring and as an *accountability tool* to determine if learning has occurred" (NEA, 2003). The National Education Association report also explained why formative assessments *for* learning are so vital to students:

> In the context of classroom assessment, however, one key purpose can be to use assessment results to inform students about themselves. *That is, classroom assessments can inform students about the continuous improvements in their achievement and permit them to feel in control of that growth. Thus, classroom*

assessments become assessments for learning. Teachers involve their students in the classroom assessment process for the express purpose of increasing their achievement (NEA, 2003).

The daunting number of academic content standards that students are expected to learn each year presents a formidable challenge to teachers.

Power Standards (Priority Standards)

The daunting number of academic content standards that studentsare expected to learn each year presents a formidable challenge to teachers whose primary responsibility it is to impart all thosestandards to their students. Teachers must also determine the progress students are making toward proficiency with these manystandards, and they need to be able to make sound decisions based on the data they collect. With so many learning objectives to teach and assess, how can teachers do this effectively?

One important way they can narrow their instruction and assessment focus is to identify the *Power Standards*: a prioritized subset of the entire list of standards that represents the essential conceptsand skills students must understand and be able to demonstrate competency in by the end of each school year, prekindergarten through grade 12 (Ainsworth, 2003a).

Educational researcher Robert Marzano provided the following data to estimate the amount of time it would take to effectivelyteach all the standards students are expected to learn by the endof high school:

- 5.6 instructional hours per day x 180 days in a typical academic year = 1,008 hours per year x 13 years = 13,104 total hours of K–12 instruction.

- Mid-continent Research for Education and Learning (McREL) identified 200 standards and 3,093 benchmarks in national- and state-level documents across 14 different subject areas.

- Classroom teachers estimated a need for 15,465 hours to adequately teach them all (Marzano, 2003, pp. 24–25).

Further, Marzano revealed a powerful reality check regarding how many of those instructional hours each school day are actually devoted to instruction of students:

- Varies widely from a low of 21 percent to a high of 69 percent

- Taking the highest estimate of 69 percent, only 9,042 hours are actually available for instruction out of the original   13,104 hours total.

- 200 standards and 3,093 benchmarks requiring 15,465 instructional hours cannot be thoroughly taught in only 9,042 hours of instructional time (Marzano, 2003, pp. 24–25).

Marzano concluded his statistics with a memorable bit of logic: "To cover all this content, you would have to change schooling fromK-12 to K-22." He recommended a fractional guideline for reducing the number of standards—"By my reckoning, we would have to cut content by about two-thirds"—and ended with a dramatic assertion: "The sheer number of standards is the biggest impedimentto implementing standards" (Marzano, 2001, p. 15).

Power Standards are *not* the only standards educators teach in any given content area. The other standards must also be taught, but a clear distinction is made as to which standards require the greatest amount of instructional time and emphasis. Vertically aligned from one grade to the next, these prioritized standards represent what all students must know and be able to do in order to be successful —in school each year, in life, and on all high-stakes assessments. Power Standards provide the laser-like focus teachers need to develop instructional units and the corresponding assessments to determine student proficiency on those essential standards.

Common formative assessments, when collaboratively designed, administered, scored, and analyzed, are directly aligned to the Power Standards *only*. Because these assessments are formative, grade-level teams of teachers can use the results to differentiate and improve instruction of those standards critical for all-round student success.

Vertical Alignment

An invaluable activity to enhance the conceptual unit building process described in step 3 and the development of common formative assessments described later in this chapter is to involve grade-level teams of teachers first in selecting and then in vertically aligning their math Power Standards. Working in grade-level teams (elementary) and course or department teams (secondary), each grade level decides the essential mathematical skills and concepts students need for success in each grade level and course. They then vertically align those selected Power Standards from one grade level to the next, both *within* each span of grades (preK–2, 3–5, 6–8, and 9–12) and then *between* each grade span (2–3, 5–6, 8–9), until there is a "vertical flow" of all the standards considered essential for students to know and be able to do by the end of high school.

Step 5: Common Formative Assessment

To accomplish this, teachers rely first upon their professional judgment and classroom experience, and use the selection criteria of endurance, leverage, and readiness for the next level of learning to make their Power Standards selections. The easiest way to do this is to consider what students need to know and be able to do to be mathematically successful (1) in school each year; (2) in life; and (3) on the annual state assessment. Beginning in one particular strand of mathematics (e.g., geometry, algebra, data, measurement, number, etc.), teachers reach initial consensus among themselves as to which standards for each individual grade are the "power" ones. Next, they cross-reference district or state standards and their annual state assessment data to check that their selections match the concepts and skills most heavily emphasized on the state test; they then modify the selections as needed. After that, they chart their selections by grade level and post them on the wall in consecutive sequence from prekindergarten through high school grades.

The preK–12 group then examines the selections from one grade to the next, looking across the charts to trace the development of key concepts and skills across the span of grade levels and courses. During their discussions, the participating teachers look for gaps from one level to the next and make changes on the charts to address specific gaps as needed.

This *gap analysis* process is extremely valuable. For example, a preK–12 team in a midwestern state was examining vertically aligned Power Standards selections in the number-sense strand. The fifth-grade team of teachers noticed an apparent break in the conceptual development of fractions, which occurred in both second and third grades. The grade 5 teachers knew that systematic development of students' understanding of fractions was a critical concept for student success at their grade level. Without the development of fractional understanding *in each and every grade* below grade 5, students would not come to grade 5 with the necessary prerequisite understanding of fractions. After this discovery was brought to everyone's attention, the teachers in grades 2 and 3 willingly revised their number-strand selections so that the flow of fractional development continued throughout all elementary years. The middle school teachers present were very encouraged by this, knowing how critical a solid understanding of fractional concepts is to student success in middle school mathematics.

The identification of preK–12 math Power Standards helps all teachers in every grade level and course know exactly which standards they must emphasize in order to develop in-depth student understanding. These Power Standards become the central focus for conceptual unit building (described in Chapter 3) and for the development of common formative assessments aligned to those conceptual units.

Readers interested in learning more about the process for identifying Power Standards, not only in math but in all content areas, will find this information fully described with accompanying district examples in *Power Standards: Identifying the Standards That Matter Most* (Ainsworth, 2003a), and in the publications of educational author and researcher, Douglas B. Reeves.

> *The identification of preK–12 math Power Standards helps all teachers in every grade level and course know exactly which standards they must emphasize in order to develop in-depth student understanding.*

Beginning with the End in Mind

Ideally, grade-level or department math teachers will collaboratively design common formative assessments to administer to all their students several times a year. Teachers can use the pre-assessment results to improve instructional planning within their own individual classrooms. Knowing—in advance—what will be required of their students on the common formative math post-assessment, they can plan the instruction, lessons, and informal classroom assessments needed to prepare students for success on that common formative post-assessment. This "backwards planning" (Wiggins & McTighe, 1998) approach will greatly assist teachers in keeping their instruction closely aligned to the common assessments.

As teachers informally assess their students throughout the conceptual unit, they will gain diagnostic information as to what their students still need to know and be able to do. This information will help them monitor and adjust instruction *before* students take the end-of-unit classroom assessment and the common formative post-assessment. If teachers use the assessment results at each stage of the process to adjust instruction as needed, these aligned classroom and grade-level assessments become extremely valuable for informing and differentiating instruction.

Designing the Common Formative Assessment

Common formative assessments can be very similar in design to the end-of-unit classroom assessments. A grade-level team of teachers that has already collaboratively designed a conceptual unit assessment for a key mathematical topic can design a similar version of that same assessment as a common formative assessment. The teachers emphasize the same key concepts and skills, but change the problems. They all administer the common assessment to their students as soon as instruction and the learning activities for the unit are completed.

More often, however, grade-level teams design a different common formative assessment that includes a blend of items, including both selected-response questions (multiple choice, short answer, matching) and constructed-response questions (Problem-Solving Task). The common assessment may also include problems from more than one math standard or strand. Whereas the classroom end-of-unit assessment (as shown in the step 3 example in Chapter 3) is more performance-based (a Problem-Solving Task), the common formative assessment may also include computation problems matched to the Power Standards targeted during one or more conceptual units. Such common assessments require students to demonstrate both their procedural understanding *and* their conceptual understanding. In this way, the assessment provides teachers with a multiple-measure insight into students' understanding.

The Implementation Sequence

Here is a recommended sequence of steps to follow when an elementary grade-level team of teachers decides to design and administer a common formative math assessment. Note that the common formative assessment is designed as both a pre- and a post-assessment, so that teachers can use the *pre*-assessment results to determine how best to meet student learning needs during the upcoming unit of instruction, and then use the *post-assessment* results at the end of the unit to measure the learning gains made by each student.

1. *Identify the math Power Standards* for each grade level and course, preK–12. (This is usually done as a district-wide process, but it can be done within an individual school. In this example, an elementary school determines its preK–5 math Power Standards.)

2. *Within grade-level teams, determine an important math topic* to teach conceptually in the classroom. Locate that topic in the identified math Power Standards.

3. *"Unwrap" those Power Standards* (as described in Chapter 3) to pinpoint the concepts and skills students need to know and be able to do.

4. *Determine the Big Ideas and Essential Questions* from the "unwrapped" Power Standards.

5. *Collaboratively design common formative pre- and post-assessments* that are aligned to one another, to evaluate student understanding of the "unwrapped" Power Standards' concepts, skills, and Big Ideas for that important topic.

6. *Design a classroom end-of-unit assessment and scoring guide* matched to the common formative assessment.

7. *Plan the classroom conceptual unit of instruction,* making sure it is aligned with the end-of-unit assessment.

8. *Administer and score the common formative pre-assessment* and analyze the results in grade-level Data Teams. (*Note: Data Teams* are collaborative teams of teachers who teach the same grade level or math course. They use a simple, five-step process

to chart student data, analyze the data, set a team goal, select effective teaching strategies, and develop an action plan. For more information on the Data Team process, please contact The Leadership and Learning Center (formerly the Center for Performance Assessment) at 1-866-399-6019 or visit its Web site at www.LeadandLearn.com).

9. *Teach the conceptual units of instruction* in each classroom. Assess informally throughout the unit and adjust instruction accordingly.

10. *Administer and score the common formative post-assessment* and analyze the results in grade-level Data Teams.

The Big Picture—How All the Practices Connect

Here is an additional sequence of steps that shows how to align the school-based common formative assessments with district and state assessments. Following that is a diagram that represents the connections between each of the practices described in this chapter (Figure 5.1). This information is relevant for all elementary- and secondary-grade teachers, math grade-level and department chairs, and school leaders, because it represents the "big-picture" alignment of preK–12 math standards and assessments and shows the connections between particular components of *Five Easy Steps* and those practices.

1. *Align common formative assessments* in each school with quarterly district benchmark assessments (elementary/secondary) and end-of-course assessments (secondary).

2. *Administer quarterly district benchmark assessments;* analyze those results (whether formative or summative) in Data Teams to inform current and future instruction and assessment.

3. *Align quarterly district benchmark and end-of-course assessments* with the annual state assessments. (*Note:* Educators do this by referencing (1) state assessment requirements, (2) current-year and prior-year school and district state test data, and (3) released state assessment items and formats from prior years. This enables the educators to better prepare students for what will be expected of them on the annual state assessments.)

Figure 5.1 shows how all these practices interconnect. Note the double-headed arrow on the elementary district benchmark assessments; this indicates that the assessments can be either formative or summative. The single-headed arrow pointing to the end-of-course secondary assessments indicates that these assessments are summative only.

Readers interested in more detailed information about the collaborative design, administration, scoring, and analysis of common formative assessments, as the centerpiece of an integrated instruction and assessment system, will find a complete description of each of these interrelated practices in *Common Formative Assessments: How to Connect Standards-Based Instruction and Assessment* (Ainsworth & Viegut, 2006).

Five Easy Steps Balanced Math Alignment Diagram

Figure 5.1

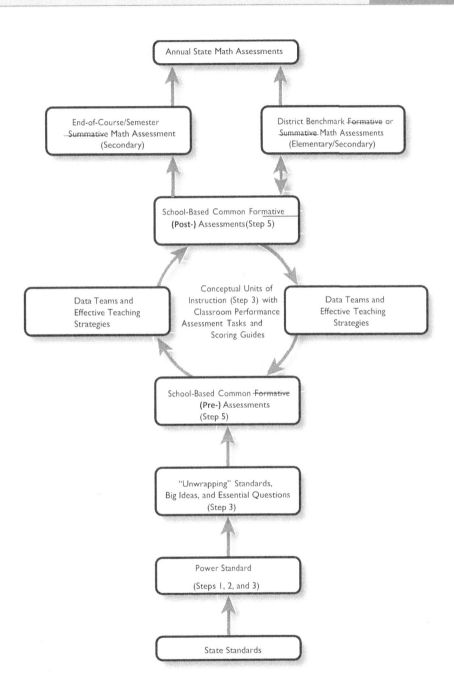

Adapted from *Common Formative Assessments: How to Connect Standards-Based Instruction and Assessment* (Ainsworth & Viegut, Corwin Press, 2006).

We recommend first "weeding the garden" of time-consuming activities that may prevent teachers from focusing on new practices that really will improve instruction and student learning.

Implementation

Today's teachers and leaders have more to do than ever before. The resistance to implementing one more professional practice, however beneficial, often proves a difficult hurdle to overcome. The key here is relevance. If teachers see the direct connection of a new practice to improvement in student learning, they are usually willing to experiment with it in their own classrooms.

We recommend first "weeding the garden" of time-consuming activities that may prevent teachers from focusing on new practicesthat really will improve instruction and student learning. Once the ground has been cleared, then introduce the new practices; allow everyone time to try them out, and then gather together to discuss their effectiveness. If teachers see firsthand the value of those recommended new practices, discussions will naturally turn to effective implementation of them within the school's established instruction and assessment culture.

An excellent way to introduce each of the *Five Easy Steps* and related practices described in these pages is to start by taking small steps. Rather than attempting to simultaneously implement each of the five steps, while at the same time identifying Power Standards and forming Data Teams, choose one of these practices and focus onunderstanding and implementing that one first. When that practiceis solidly in place, implement the next one; then continue through the remaining practices. In this way, teachers can effectively evaluatethe worth of each of these interdependent practices. In less time than initially expected, all of these practices can put be in place andstart working together to improve student achievement in math!

Benefits

Common formative assessments can greatly improve instruction and corresponding student achievement. Among their several important benefits are:

Regular and timely feedback regarding student attainment of the most essential math standards, so teachers can better meet the learning needs of all students

Multiple-measure assessments that allow students to demonstrate their understanding in a variety of formats

Ongoing collaboration opportunities for primary grade-level teachers

Consistent expectations within a grade level and within a grade span regarding standards, instruction, and assessment priorities

Established criteria for proficiency, to be met within each individual classroom, grade level, school, and district

Deliberate preparation for students to be successful through the intentional alignment of classroom and school assessments with external district and state assessments

Teachers well know that it always takes a lot of work to institute any new program or practice. The positive results to be gained by students indeed justify the time and effort required by the adults in the system to achieve those results. As you implement—over time—each of the *Five Easy Steps to a Balanced Math Program*, you will see for yourself a dramatic increase in student achievement. Even more importantly, you are likely to witness students' perceptions of their ability to "do math" shifting slowly but surely in the right direction. How rewarding it is for hard-working teachers to see students beginning to think of themselves as mathematically powerful!

In the next three chapters, we show the application of the *Five Easy Steps* in each of the primary grades: kindergarten, grade 1, and grade 2.

Reader's Assignment

Discuss these ideas with grade-level colleagues. Talk with your administrator to request collaborative planning time to first identify the math Power Standards and then develop a common formative assessment matched to a particular grade-level math topic of importance. Progressing at a pace appropriate for you and your colleagues, follow the suggested sequence of steps described in this chapter for designing common formative assessments.

PART TWO

Inside the
Primary Classroom

Inside the Kindergarten Classroom

In this chapter, we show the application of the five steps of the balanced math program model in a kindergarten classroom. The examples provided illustrate Math Review, Mental Math, problem solving, and a Conceptual Understanding Unit. In addition, we have included information regarding the teaching of math facts. We hope these grade-specific examples will benefit kindergarten teachers in implementing these important balanced math program steps!

Step 1: Kindergarten Computational Skills (Math Review and Mental Math)

The Math Review Template

Math Review, as described in Chapter 1, occurs daily at the beginning of math time. Using the Math Review template, teachers write the types of problems on the board and provide students with an individual worksheet of the problems on which to show their work.

1. Build the number 8.	2. ○○□ ○○□ — — —	3. What month comes before November?
Number	Pattern	Measurement

To complete Math Review within the allotted time frame, however, we suggest fully processing only one or two different problems each day.

Teaching Sequence.

1. Write the selected problems on a chart or on the board and provide each student with an individual worksheet.

2. Explain the directions for each problem.

3. Ask students to use manipulatives to solve the problems.

4. Complete each problem, one at a time, to diagnose student understanding.

Processing Sequence.

In this section are suggested strategies teachers can emphasize, during the processing of Math Review problems, to develop students' number sense and mathematical reasoning. Teachers can refer to these processing examples when developing their own strategies for processing Math Review problems. To complete Math Review within the allotted time frame, however, we suggest fully processing only one or two different problems each day. Provide just the answers for the others. There is not enough time to use every processing strategy for every problem every day, but do be sure to include *all* of these processing strategies over the course of each week.

1. For the **Number** problem—"Build the number 8"—students use manipulatives to show the quantity of 8:

   • Ask students to build one more than 8 and say the number that is represented.

   • Ask students to build one less than 8, two more than 8, two less than 8, and so on, and say the numbers that are represented. Progress in difficulty as the school year continues.

2. For the **Pattern** problem, students draw or use manipulatives to show the next three parts of the pattern.

   - Tell students that the pattern can be labeled "AAB" in mathematics

   - Ask students to show the next part of the pattern after that

   - Ask students where they see patterns outside of school

3. For the **Measurement** problem—"What month comes before November?"—students chorally say the month before November or each student tells a neighbor.

   - Ask students what month comes after November

   - Say the months of the year together

The Math Review Quiz

The Math Review Quiz that becomes a weekly assessment of students' computational understanding beginning in grade 1 is not, in our experience, appropriate for kindergarten students. However, teachers are certainly able to assess students informally to determine their proficiency with the types of problems being presented daily during Math Review.

Mental Math

Mental Math should be matched to the content of Math Review. Regular practice will help develop students' number sense. Here are three examples of Mental Math problems that are appropriate for kindergarten, with incremental answers provided. The word "equals" signals students to say or write the answer (provided in the last parenthetical of the problem in each of the following examples). Note also the Mental Math themes for each particular type of problem. Kindergarten teachers may use these examples as guidelines for developing their own Mental Math problems.

EXAMPLES

"Start with one more than five (**6**); add two more (**8**); equals_____."
(Theme: one more than, two more than)

"Start with the number of days in a week (**7**); add three more (**10**); equals_____."
(Themes: measurement; combinations that make 10)

"Start with five (**5**); double it (**10**); add one more (**11**); equals_____."
(Theme: doubles plus one)

Step 2: Kindergarten Problem Solving

The Problem-Solving Teaching Sequenceto Follow Throughout the Year

1. The teacher introduces the selected problem.

2. Students, working alone or with a partner, try to solve the problem using manipulatives. Teachers encourage students to make a graphic representation of the solution to the problem using words, pictures, and/or numbers.

3. Students share with the class their ideas of how they worked on the problem.

4. The teacher records students' ideas on chart paper (the class Data Sheet).

5. The teacher and students solve the problem together and agree on a solution.

6. The teacher and students do a write-up together. With student input, the teacher writes several sentences describing the sequence that was followed to solve the problem.

Sample Kindergarten Problem-Solving Task

The following is a sample Problem-Solving Task for the strand or standard of *algebra and functions*. It is designed to match the Conceptual Understanding Unit shown in step 3.

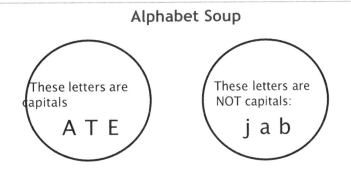

Alphabet Soup

These letters are capitals

A T E

These letters are NOT capitals:

j a b

Circle letters that are capitals.

| f | B | X | C | D | o | i | T | L |
| q | r | W | s | M | Y | t | R | P |

Name some of your own capitals.

Explain why you know they are capitals.

Source: Ventura Unified Mathematics Sampler K–12; adapted from "Alphabet Soup" developed by Conejo Unified School District, Conejo, California.

Transition During the School Year

1. *Beginning of the year*—do the problem-solving sequence (listed earlier) as a whole class.

2. *Middle of the year*—continue doing the problem-solving process together, but begin having students record their own thinking on individual Data Sheets.

3. *End of the year*—students make their own Data Sheets and write one or two sentences describing their process.

Step 3: Kindergarten Conceptual Understanding

The following is a sample Conceptual Understanding Unit matched to the strand or standard of *algebra and functions*. It was selected to align with the Problem-Solving Task shown in step 2.

Grade Level: Kindergarten

Conceptual Unit Focus: Algebra and functions

Standards and Indicators Matched to Unit Focus:

[Here teachers list and "unwrap" the full text of the relevant standard and indicators from individual district or state documents for the selected topic. *Source:* California Standards, Algebra and Functions, Section 1, Item 1.1; Mathematical Reasoning, Section 2, Item 2.1.]

"Unwrapped" Concepts: Need to Know about Algebra and Functions

❑ Attribute
❑ Objects, concrete objects
❑ Grouping
❑ Pictorial representation

Step 3: Kindergarten Conceptual Understanding

❏ Data

❏ Picture graphs

Skills: Be Able to Do:

❏ Identify (objects)

❏ Sort (objects)

❏ Classify (objects)

❏ Explain (reasoning)

❏ Collect (data)

❏ Organize (information)

Topics or Context:

❏ Mathematics textbook

❏ Other resource materials (to be decided by teachers)

Big Ideas:

1. Objects can be compared based on their attributes.

2. Objects can be sorted by using a rule.

3. Relationships can be seen in organized information.

Essential Questions:

1. How can objects be compared?

2. How can objects be sorted?

3. What can we learn from organized information?

End-of-Unit Assessment:

Teacher preparation: Gather 20 buttons of differing sizes, shapes, colors, and unique characteristics, such as number of holes or different textures.

Directions: The student sorts the buttons into groups and answers the following three questions:

1. Which buttons go together?

2. How did you sort the buttons?

3. Why did you put these buttons together?

Students then graph their sorted buttons on a graph mat. The teacher records student graphing ona record sheet.

Scoring Guide:

Exemplary:

- ❏ All "Proficient" criteria *plus*:
- ❏ Justifies sort with a rule
- ❏ Multiple descriptions of the graph

Proficient:

- ❏ Sorts buttons into appropriate groups
- ❏ Represents sort in graph form
- ❏ Describes graph

Progressing:

- ❏ Student work meets 2 of the "Proficient" criteria

Beginning:

- ❏ Student work meets fewer than 2 of the "Proficient" criteria
- ❏ Assessment task to be repeated after remediation

Self-Evaluation_____

Teacher's Evaluation _____

Source: K–7 Math Performance Task binder. Special thanks to the San Diego County Office of Education and the K–2 Performance Assessment Team for permission to reprint this assessment.

Step 4: Kindergarten Mastery of Math Facts

An effective way to practice math facts is through the processing of Math Review and by involving students in daily Mental Math activities. Kindergarten students need lots of experience in developing their number sense. This will greatly help them to be successful in remembering their math facts as they progress through elementary school. Math Review and Mental Math provide students with repeated emphasis on the following number-sense patterns:

The quantity of a number

How to correctly say a number

One more than a number

Doubles

Addition facts that make five

Addition facts that make ten

Step 5: Common Formative Assessment

As described in Chapter 5, common formative assessments administered to all students in the grade level can be identical or very similar in design to the end-of-unit classroom assessment. The grade-level team of teachers that has already collaboratively designed a conceptual unit assessment for a key mathematical topic can simply use a similar assessment as the common formative assessment. However, whereas the classroom end-of-unit assessment is typically more performance-based (a Problem-Solving Task), the common formative assessment may additionally include computation problems or a blend of selected-response and constructed-response items.

Common formative assessments may also address standards other than those targeted during any one particular conceptual unit. Nevertheless, it is important to emphasize that common formative assessments are primarily designed to evaluate student proficiency on the math Power Standards *only.* Because there are so many variables to take into consideration when designing a common formative math assessment, we chose not to includea grade-level sample matched only to the particular math focus topic represented in steps 2 and 3.

Decisions as to the design, administration, scoring, analysis, and frequency of common formative assessments, to measure ongoing student understanding of particular math Power Standards, are left to the collaborative team of teachers. For guidelines in this regard, please refer again to Chapter 5.

Inside the Grade 1 Classroom

In this chapter, we show the application of the five steps of the balanced math program model in a grade 1 classroom. The examples provided illustrate Math Review, Mental Math, problem solving, and a Conceptual Understanding Unit. In addition, we have included information regarding the teaching of math facts. We hope these grade-specific examples will benefit first-grade teachers in implementing these important balanced math program steps!

Step 1: First-Grade Computational Skills (Math Review and Mental Math)

The Math Review Template

Math Review, as described in Chapter 1, occurs daily at the beginning of math time. First-grade teachers may want to begin the school year with three problems and then transition to five problems halfway through the year. First-graders typically begin doing the Math Review problems as a whole class, and then work toward completing the problems independently. Using the Math Review template, teachers write the problems on the board and either have students copy the problems or prepare an individual worksheet for each student.

1. 6___8____10 Number	**2.** 3+ ____ = 5 4 +___ = 5 Addition	**3.** 2, 4, 6, ___ ,_____,_____, Pattern
4. Name and describe.  Geometry	**5.** ___Days = 1 week ____ months = 1 year Measurement	**6.** Bonus

Teaching Sequence at Beginning of School Year.

1. Write the selected number of problems on a chart or on the board and provide each student with an individual worksheet.

2. Explain the directions for each problem.

3. Ask students to use manipulatives to solve the problems.

4. Complete each problem, one at a time, to diagnose student understanding.

Processing Sequence.

In this section are suggested strategies teachers can emphasize, during the processing of Math Review problems, to develop students' number sense and mathematical reasoning. Teachers can refer to these processing examples when developing their own strategies for processing Math Review problems. To complete Math Review within the allotted time frame, however, we suggest fully processing only two or three different problems each day. Provide just the answers for the others. There is not enough time to use every processing strategy for every problem every day, but do be sure to include *all* of these processing strategies over the course of each week. For the bonus problem, ask those students who solved it to orally state their answer along with a brief description of how they solved it.

1. For the **Number** problem:

   - Ask students what the missing numbers are

   - Say the entire sequence together (6, 7, 8, 9, 10)

   - Ask students what number comes before 6; what number comes after 10; what number is 2 more than 10; what number is 2 less than 6; and so on

2. For the **Addition** problem:

   - Ask students to explain how they found their answers

   - Remind students about the five-frame

   - Ask students what other numbers combine to make 5

3. For the **Pattern** problem:

   - Ask students what pattern they see (counting by 2s)

   - Ask students for the next three numbers in the sequence

   - Count chorally by 2s to 20 or 30

   - Ask what else students know about the numbers in the sequence (that the numbers are even)

4. For the **Geometry** problem:

- Ask students what they noticed about the shape (they should notice three sides, three angles, and that the angles are less than a right angle)

- Ask students to compare triangles to other shapes they know. Point out that "tri-" means "three," so "triangle" means "three angles."

5. For the **Measurement** problem:

- Ask students how many days are in the week

- Say the days of the week together

- Ask how many days there are in two weeks

- Ask how many months are in one year

- Say the names of the months together

- Ask how many months there are in two years

The Math Review Quiz

The Math Review Quiz becomes a weekly assessment of students' computational understanding beginning in grade 1. Its purpose is to assess students on a regular basis to determine their proficiency with the types of problems they are practicing daily during Math Review. Note that there are *two* problems for each type of daily problem.

1. 7,_____,_____, 10

2. 11,_____, _____

3. 1 +_____ = 5

4. 2 + _____ = 5

Step 1: First-Grade Computational Skills
     (Math Review and Mental Math)

5. 2,_____, 6, 8, _____

6. 12, 14,_____, _____

7. Name and describe △

8. Name and describe ▢

9. _____ days = 2 weeks

10. _____ months = 2 years

Mental Math

Mental Math should be matched to the content of Math Review. Regular practice will help develop students' number sense. Here are three examples of Mental Math problems that are appropriate for grade 1, with incremental answers provided. The word "equals" signals students to say or write the answer (provided in the last parenthetical of the problem in each of the following examples). Note also the Mental Math themes for each particular type of problem. First-grade teachers may use these examples as guidelines for developing their own Mental Math problems.

EXAMPLES

"Start with 10 + 2 **(12)**; add 2 **(14)**; equals_____."
(Theme: counting by 2s)

"Start with 3 + 2 **(5)**; subtract 3 **(2)**; double the answer **(4)**; equals_____."
(Themes: part-part-whole; doubles)

"Start with the number of days in a week **(7)**; add the number of months in a year **(19)**; add one more **(20)**; equals_____."
(Themes: measurement; general knowledge)

Step 2: First-Grade Problem Solving

The Problem-Solving Teaching Sequence for the Beginning of the School Year

1. The teacher introduces the selected problem.

2. Students, working alone or with a partner, try to solve the problem using manipulatives. Teachers encourage students to make a graphic representation of the solution to the problem using words, pictures, and/or numbers.

3. Students share with the class their ideas of how they worked on the problem.

4. The teacher records students' ideas on chart paper (the class Data Sheet).

5. Students copy the class Data Sheet.

6. The teacher and students solve the problem together and agree on a solution.

7. The teacher and students do a write-up together. With student input, the teacher writes several sentences describing the sequence that was followed to solve the problem.

8. Students copy the class write-up using the primary-grades Problem-Solving Task Write-Up Guide.

The Problem-Solving Teaching Sequence for the Middle of the School Year

1. Teacher and students solve the given problem together.

2. Students begin to work in small, cooperative groups to solve the given problem.

3. In each group, students create a Data Sheet and a write-up.

4. The whole class and the teacher agree on the solution and complete a class write-up together.

5. Students compare their small-group write-ups to the whole-class write-up and edit as needed so that they match.

The Problem-Solving Teaching Sequence for the End of the School Year

1. Students attempt the entire process independently.

2. Teachers emphasize that there is more than one way to solve the problem.

3. Teachers guide students to follow the same process independently that they have practiced together as a class and in small groups.

Sample Grade 1 Problem-Solving Task

The following is a sample Problem-Solving Task for the strand or standard of *number sense and computation.* It is designed to match the Conceptual Understanding Unit shown in step 3.

On the tray of cookies, there are 10 jellybean, 15 molasses, 5 sugar, and 4 chocolate chip. You have 4 pennies, 1 nickel, and 1 dime. What different kinds of cookies can you buy? You need to spend **all** your money.

Make a list of the possible ways.

Explain why you think your ways make sense.

Source: Ventura Unified Mathematics Sampler K–12, Ventura, CA.

Step 3: First-Grade Conceptual Understanding

The following is a sample Conceptual Understanding Unit matched to the strand or standard of *number sense and computation.* It was selected to align with the Problem-Solving Task shown in step 2. Note that the assessment is in two parts. The first part is *constructed-response* and will be evaluated with a task-specific rubric or scoring guide. The second part is *selected-response* and will be evaluated by a 10-point or percentage scale.

Grade Level: Grade 1

Conceptual Unit Focus: Money

Standards and Indicators Matched to Unit Focus:

[Here teachers list and "unwrap" the full text of the relevant standard and indicators from individual district or state documents for the selected topic. *Source:* Virginia Standards of Learning 1.10A, B, C, D, ND.]

"Unwrapped" Skills Matched to Concepts:

❑ Trade/use _____
    Different sets of coins with the same value to $1.00

❑ Identify
    Number of pennies   5 cents, 10 cents, and 25 cents
    Value of each coin
    Coins needed to buy items

❑ Sort
    A collection of pennies, nickels, dimes, or quarters to $1.00
    Pennies by ones, nickels by fives, and dimes by tens
    Groups of coins composed of mixed combinations to $1.00

❑ Compare
    Value of sets of mixed coins

Topics or Context:

❑ Mathematics textbook

❑ Other resource materials (to be decided by teachers)

Big Ideas:

1. Money can be coins used to buy items.

2. Coins have different sizes and values.

3. Different sets of coins can have the same value.

Essential Questions:

1. What is money and how do we use it?

2. How is the size of the coin related to its value?

3. How many ways can you choose coins to equal a given amount?

End-of-Unit Assessment, Part I — Performance Assessment:

Summary: Given a set of coins, the student will identify the coins, determine the amount, show another way to make the same amount, and decide which items can be bought.

Directions:

1. Students are given coins in a cup. They draw a picture of the coins and tell how many of each type of coin they have (e.g., penny, penny, penny, nickel 3 pennies and 1 nickel).

2. Using the coins that are in their cups, students will use "counting on" to get the total value of the coins.

3. Students draw a picture of another set of coins to equal the amount of the coins they have in their cups.

4. An activity sheet showing 10 pictures of items with price tags is passed out to each student. Each student circles the pictures of the items that can be bought with the money in his or her cup.

Step 3: First-Grade Conceptual Understanding

Constructed-Assessment Scoring Guide:

Exemplary:

- ❏ All "Proficient" criteria *plus*:
- ❏ Coins drawn relative to actual size
- ❏ Correct number sentence written for total value of coins

Proficient:

- ❏ All coins labeled correctly
- ❏ Correct total value given
- ❏ Correct number written for quantity of types of coins
- ❏ Drawings represent quantity of coins equal to coins given

Progressing:

- ❏ Student work meets 3 of the 4 "Proficient" criteria

Beginning:

- ❏ Student work meets fewer than 3 of the "Proficient" criteria
- ❏ Assessment task to be repeated after remediation
- ❏

End-of-Unit Assessment, Part II— Selected-Response Written at Knowledge/Application Level and Higher:

1. A_____is worth 5 cents.

   a. dime

   b. nickel

   c. penny

2. A quarter is worth_____ .

   a. 10 cents

   b. 1 cent

   c. 25 cents

3. A penny, nickel, and dime are worth_____ .

   a. 17 cents

   b. 16 cents

   c. 15 cents

4. You have 1 quarter, 1 dime, and 2 pennies. You can buy a toy that costs _____ _.

   a. 50 cents

   b. 31 cents

   c. 39 cents

5. You get 10 cents a week. How much will you have in 5 weeks?

   a. 50 cents

   b. 25 cents

   c. 20 cents

6. Which coin is worth more?

   a. a penny

   b. a quarter

   c. a dime

7. How many pennies does it take to make $1.00?

   a. 10

   b. 100

   c. 50

8. Which group of coins is worth 23 cents?

   a. 1 nickel and 1 quarter

   b. 1 nickel, 1 dime, and 2 pennies

   c. 2 nickels, 1 dime, and 3 pennies

   d.

Source: Submitted anonymously from Norfolk Public Schools, Norfolk, VA.

Self-Evaluation_____

Teacher's Evaluation _____

Step 4: First-Grade Mastery of Math Facts

An effective way to practice math facts is through the processing of Math Review and by involving students in daily Mental Math activities. First-grade students should continue practice with number-sense patterns that were first introduced and developed in kindergarten:

The quantity of a number

How to correctly say a number

One more than a number

Doubles

Addition facts that make five

Addition facts that make ten

In addition, first-graders need repeated practice with the following concepts, skills, and strategies:

Part-part-whole relationships (fact-family groups)

Anchors of 5 and 10 (five-frame and ten-frame)

Counting by a given number (2s, 5s, 10s)

Two more and two less than a number

Understanding that addition and subtraction are inverse operations

Step 5: Common Formative Assessment

As described in Chapter 5, common formative assessments administered to all students in the grade level can be identical or very similar in design to the end-of-unit classroom assessment. The grade-level team of teachers that has already collaboratively designed a conceptual unit assessment for a key mathematical topic can simply use a similar assessment as the common formative assessment. However, whereas the classroom end-of-unit assessment is typically more performance-based (a Problem-Solving Task), the common formative assessment may additionally include computation problems or a blend of selected-response and constructed-response items.

Common formative assessments may also address standards other than those targeted during any one particular conceptual unit. Nevertheless, it is important to emphasize that common formative assessments are primarily designed to evaluate student proficiency of the math Power Standards *only.* Because there are so many variables to take into consideration when designing a common formative math assessment, we chose not to include a grade-level sample matched only to the particular math focus topic represented in steps 2 and 3.

Decisions as to the design, administration, scoring, analysis, and frequency of common formative assessments, to measure ongoing student understanding of particular math Power Standards, are left to the collaborative team of teachers. For guidelines in this regard, please refer again to Chapter 5.

Inside the Grade 2 Classroom

CHAPTER 8

In this chapter, we show the application of the five steps of the balanced math program model in a grade 2 classroom. The examples provided illustrate Math Review, Mental Math, problem solving, and a Conceptual Understanding Unit. In addition, we have included information regarding the teaching of math facts. We hope these grade-specific examples will benefit second-grade teachers in implementing these important balanced math program steps!

Step 1: Second-Grade Computational Skills (Math Review and Mental Math)

The Math Review Template

Math Review, as described in Chapter 1, occurs daily at the beginning of math time. Second-graders typically complete the five problems independently. However, teachers will certainly need to make whatever modifications are necessary to ensure that students can be successful working independently.

Using the Math Review template, teachers write the problems on the board and either have students copy the problems or prepare an individual worksheet for each student.

1. 21,__, __, 24	**2.** 23 +36	**3.** 20 +8
Place Value	Addition	Subtraction

4. Different coins that make $.75.	**5.** ___ inches = 1 foot ____ inches = 3 feet	**6.**
Money Unit	Measurement	Bonus

Processing Sequence.

In this section are suggested strategies teachers can emphasize, during the processing of Math Review problems, to develop students' number sense and mathematical reasoning. Teachers can refer to these processing examples when developing their own strategies for processing Math Review problems. To complete Math Review within the allotted time frame, however, we suggest fully processing only two or three different problems each day. Provide just the answers for the others. There is not enough time to use every processing strategy for every problem every day, but do be sure to include *all* of these processing strategies over the course of each week. For the bonus problem, ask those students who solved it to orally state their answer along with a brief description of how they solved it.

Step 1: Second-Grade Computational Skills (Math Review and Mental Math)

1. For the **Place Value** problem:

    • Ask students what the missing numbers are

    • Say the entire sequence together (21, 22, 23, 24)

    • Ask students what is 5 more than 24; 10 more than 24; 5 less than 21; 10 less than 21; and so on

    • Ask students what they know about a two-place number (made up of tens and ones)

2. For the **Addition** problem:

    • Ask students what a reasonable answer or good estimate would be (possible responses: 20+40= 60; a number less than 60; a number close to 60)

    • Ask students to try to solve the problem mentally

    • Ask students to share their methods

    • Show the procedure

    • Show another way to think about the problem (e.g., 20 +30 =50+ (6+ 3)= 59) to help students develop their number sense

3. For the **Subtraction** problem:

    • Ask students what a reasonable answer would be (20 - 10 =10, so the answer should be more than 10 because they rounded 8 to 10)

    • Have students compute the problem mentally and share their methods with the rest of the class

    • Show students the strategy of counting up through 10 (8+ 2=10; 10+ 10= 20; 10+ 2= 12)

    • Discuss strategy of "think addition" (8 +___ =20)

4. For the **Money Unit** problem:

- Ask students to share different ways to make $.75

- Count together the combinations of coins suggested

5. For the **Measurement** problem:

- Ask students how many inches are in one foot; how many in two feet

- Ask what things they know of that are close in length to an inch; a foot; two feet

The Math Review Quiz

First introduced in grade 1, the Math Review Quiz continues as a weekly assessment of students' computational understanding in grade 2. Its purpose is to assess students on a regular basis to determine their proficiency with the types of problems they are practicing daily during Math Review. Note that there are *two* problems for each type of daily problem.

1. 27, 28,_____, _____

2. 19,_____,_____, 22

3. 24 + 21   _____

4. 35 + 42   _____

5. 30 - 9   _____

6. 40 - 6   _____

7. One way to make $.80

8. Another way to make $.80

9. _____ inches = 3 feet

10. _____ inches = 2 feet

Mental Math

Mental Math should be matched to the content of Math Review. Regular practice will help develop students' number sense. Here are three examples of Mental Math problems that are appropriate for grade 2, with incremental answers provided. The word "equals" signals students to say or write the answer (provided in the last parenthetical of the problem in each of the following examples). Note also the Mental Math themes for each particular type of problem. Second-grade teachers may use these examples as guidelines for developing their own Mental Math problems.

EXAMPLES

"Start with $7+5$ **(12)**; double the sum **(24)**; add 6 **(30)**; doublethat answer **(60)**; equals___."
(Themes: doubles; combinations that make 10)

"Start with $6+8$ **(14)**; subtract 7 **(7)**; double the answer **(14)**; subtract 8 **(6)**; double the answer **(12)**; add 2 **(14)**; equals___."
(Themes: part-part-whole with the quantity 14)

"Start with the number of inches in a foot **(12)**; subtract 6 **(6)**; double the answer **(12)**; double the answer again **(24)**; subtractthe number of inches in 2 feet **(0)**; equals _____."

(Themes: measurement; doubling)

Step 2: Second-Grade Problem Solving

The Problem-Solving Teaching Sequence for the Beginning and Middle of the School Year

1. The teacher introduces the selected problem.

2. Teacher and students solve the given problem together.

3. Students begin to work in small, cooperative groups to solve the given problem.

4. In their groups, students create a Data Sheet (the mathematical work they did to solve the problem) and a write-up (the written explanation of their mathematical thinking and problem-solving process).

5. Whole class and teacher agree on the solution and complete a class write-up together.

6. Students compare their cooperative-group write-ups to the whole-class write-up and edit as needed so that they match.

The Problem-Solving Teaching Sequence for the End of the School Year

1. Students complete the entire process independently.

2. Teacher provides opportunity for student reflection and revision.

Sample Grade 2 Problem-Solving Task

The following is a sample Problem-Solving Task for the strand or standard of *algebra and functions* and *problem solving*. It was selected to align with the Conceptual Understanding Unit shown in step 3.

Wheels

Curious George collected bicycle and tricycle wheels. He had already found 6 wheels and then he found 3 more.

Draw a picture of how many bicycles and tricycles George could make using all the wheels he collected. Include a math sentence that matches your drawing.

Can you draw a picture to show that there might be more than one answer and then explain why?

Source: Ventura Unified Mathematics Sampler K–12, Ventura, CA.

Step 3: Second-Grade Conceptual Understanding

The following is a sample Conceptual Understanding Unit matched to the strand or standard of *algebra and functions,* and *problem solving.* It was selected to align with the Problem-Solving Task shown in step 2.

Grade Level: Grade 2

Conceptual Unit Focus: Algebra and functions; problem solving

Standards and Indicators Matched to Unit Focus:

[Here teachers list and "unwrap" the full text of the relevant standard and indicators from individual district or state documents for the selected topic. *Source:* California Standards Algebra and Functions, Section 1, Item 1.2; Mathematical Reasoning, Section 1, Items 1.1 and 1.2; Section 2, Item 2.2; Number Sense, Section 5, Item 5.1.]

"Unwrapped" Concepts: Need to Know about Algebra and Functions; Problem Solving:

❏ Number relationships
  o Problems
  o Calculations
  o Addition
  o Subtraction
❏ Decisions
  o Approach
  o Reasoning
  o Validity
  o Results
  o Strategies
❏ Manipulatives
  o Sketches

Step 3: Second-Grade Conceptual Understanding

- o Money
- o Materials
- o Tools

<u>Skills</u>: Be Able to <u>Do</u>:

- ❑ Model (number relationships)
- ❑ Represent (number relationships)
- ❑ Interpret (number relationships)
- ❑ Create (problems)
- ❑ Solve (problems)
- ❑ Justify (reasoning)
- ❑ Decide (about approach, materials, strategies)
- ❑ Use (tools)
- ❑ Check (validity of results)

Topics or Context:

- ❑ Mathematics textbook
- ❑ Other resource materials (to be decided by teachers)

Big Ideas:

1. Problems can be solved using different strategies.
2. Addition and subtraction can be used to find an amount of money.
3. Pictures and manipulatives can be used to solve problems.
4. Coins can be grouped in different ways to create an amount of money.

Essential Questions:

1. What can help us solve problems?
2. Which math operations can help us find certain amounts of money?
3. Why do we use pictures and manipulatives in math?
4. Why do we group coins together?

End-of-Unit Assessment:

Your sister has 7 coins in her pocket. She has at least one of each coin: quarter, dime, nickel, and penny. How much money could she have? Use words, pictures, and/or numbers to solve the problem. Show as many solutions as you can. Write the number sentence for each of your solutions.

Source: K–7 Math Performance Task Binder. Special thanks to the San Diego County Office of Education and the K–2 Performance Assessment Team for permission to reprint this assessment.

Scoring Guide

Exemplary:

❑ All "Proficient" criteria *plus*:

❑ More than 6 possible correct solutions

❑ Correct number sentences written for additional solutions

Proficient:

❑ Words, pictures, and/or numbers used to solve problem

❑ At least 6 possible correct solutions

❑ Correct number sentence written for each solution

❑ Solutions are in organized list

Progressing:

❑ Student work meets 3 of the "Proficient" criteria

Beginning:

❑ Student work meets fewer than 3 of the "Proficient" criteria

❑ Assessment task to be repeated after remediation

Self-Evaluation_____

Teacher's Evaluation _____

Step 4: Second-Grade Mastery of Math Facts

An effective way to practice math facts is through the processing of Math Review and by involving students in daily Mental Math activities. Second-grade students should continue practice with number-sense patterns that were developed in kindergarten and first grade:

Kindergarten

The quantity of a number

How to correctly say a number

One more than a number

Doubles

Addition facts that make five

Addition facts that make ten

First Grade

Part-part-whole relationships (fact-family groups)

Anchors of 5 and 10 (five-frame and ten-frame)

Counting by a given number (2s, 5s, 10s)

Two more and two less than a number

Understanding that addition and subtraction are inverse operations

Second graders also need continuing opportunities to develop effective strategies to recall the answers to part-part-whole relationships in addition (5 3 8; 3 5 8; 6 2 8; 2 6 8; and so on). They should develop a strong foundation with addition facts that will allow them to use the strategy of "think addition" for subtraction. For other strategies, refer again to Chapter 4.

Step 5: Common Formative Assessment

As described in Chapter 5, common formative assessments administered to all students in the grade level can be identical or very similar in design to the end-of-unit classroom assessment. The grade-level team of teachers that has already collaboratively designed a conceptual unit assessment for a key mathematical topic can simply use a similar assessment as the common formative assessment. However, whereas the classroom end-of-unit assessment is typically more performance-based (a Problem-Solving Task), the common formative assessment may additionally include computation problems or a blend of selected-response and constructed-response items.

Common formative assessments may also address standards other than those targeted during any one particular conceptual unit. Nevertheless, it is important to emphasize that common formative assessments are primarily designed to evaluate student proficiency of the math Power Standards *only*. Because there are so many variables to take into consideration when designing a common formative math assessment, we chose not to include a grade-level sample matched only to the particular math focus topic represented in steps 2 and 3.

Step 5: Common Formative Assessment

Decisions as to the design, administration, scoring, analysis, and frequency of common formative assessments, to measure ongoing student understanding of particular math Power Standards, are left to the collaborative team of teachers. For guidelines in this regard, please refer again to Chapter 5.

PART THREE

Resources for Implementation

Putting It All Together: Time Management and Frequently Asked Questions

So there you have it: the five steps to implementing a balanced math program! Even though it will certainly take time and perseverance to incorporate each of these steps into the math instruction and assessment practices of your school, the steps will become easier as teachers deepen their understanding of the program through firsthand experience.

This chapter is divided into two sections. In the first, we offer practical suggestions for time management that have proven effective. In the second, we share the questions most frequently asked by teachers during Five Easy Steps *workshops and provide the answers to address them.*

Part 1: Time Management

Regardless of whether they teach a self-contained class of elementary-grade children or several sections of students in a secondary setting, classroom teachers face the uncompromising time constraints of the ever-ticking clock. An elementary teacher is responsible for teaching the standards in all the academic content areas, and must continually adjust the daily schedule to meet the demands of doing so. The time allotment for mathematics often varies according to the individual school or grade level and the number of instructional minutes mandated by the school district. As a general rule of thumb, however, elementary teachers devote about 60 to 75 minutes to math 5 days each week. Because they are typically with the same students all day, they can decide whether to schedule math in the morning or the afternoon.

> *We hope that you, as a primary-grade math teacher, are concluding your study of this book with new ideas for maximizing the time available for math instruction and assessment in your particular situation.*

A secondary-grade math teacher may have only one content area to focus on, but must strive to meet the needs of several sections of students, each within a fixed time frame of 54 minutes or less. Recognition of the need for more instructional time is one of the reasons why so many middle schools and high schools are moving to a block or modified block schedule. Still, the challenge is great for those who decide to incorporate computational practice, problem-solving experiences, and lessons that emphasize conceptual understanding (as described in Chapters 1, 2, and 3, respectively) within the preset time limits of each day's schedule.

We hope that you, as a primary-grade math teacher, are concluding your study of this book with new ideas for maximizing the time available for math instruction and assessment in your particular situation. The following is a suggested schedule for implementing the *Five Easy Steps* in a second-grade classroom. Kindergarten and grade 1 teachers can modify this sample schedule to meet their own needs.

A Second-Grade Math Schedule

This sample second-grade math schedule shows how to implement the first four steps of our balanced math program (computational skills, problem solving, conceptual understanding, and mastery of math facts). A teacher decides to schedule math for 65 minutes daily, with an additional 10 minutes on Friday to complete her conceptual-understanding assessment activities. Her initial focus is on Math Review and Mental Math (step 1) and a Conceptual Understanding Unit of instruction (step 3). Because she wants the problem-solving activities (step 2) to reflect application of the current conceptual unit, she is not yet ready to introduce the related Problem-Solving Task; that will begin in week three.

Part 1: Time Management

Nor will she begin the mastery of math facts (step 4) accountability program yet: she wants to first explain this to parents at a Back-to-School Night (or by means of a letter, if the school year is already well under way), and introduce the math-facts step to students after that. This is an example of how a teacher might allocate math time each day during the first four weeks of implementation.

Grade 2 Math Schedule

Weeks One and Two

Monday through Thursday

Math Review —10 minutes

Process Math Review—10 minutes

Mental Math —5 minutes

Conceptual Unit—35 minutes

Assign homework (conceptual unit extension or computational skills practice)— 5 minutes

Total minutes: 65 daily

Friday: Assessment Day

Math Review Quiz—30 minutes

Score quiz together (optional)—10 minutes

Math Review self-reflection (optional, but recommended)—
5 minutes

Assessment of week's conceptual unit learning — 30 minutes OR

Conceptual lesson game/activity that supports unit — 30 minutes

Total minutes: 60 to 75

We recommend introducing the Problem-Solving Task during the third week of the school year, or the third week after beginning steps 1 and 3 of the balanced math program in the classroom. This will provide a full two weeks to establish the sequence of

Math Review, Mental Math, and the Conceptual Understanding Unit with students. It will also provide students with two weeks of instruction geared to the conceptual unit focus. By then students will be ready to apply their conceptual understanding to a problem-solving situation.

The following schedule incorporates the problem-solving activities described in Chapter 2. Notice the difference in the instructional sequence as compared with weeks one and two. The Problem-Solving Task replaces the conceptual unit lesson on Monday, Tuesday, and Wednesday, but it *applies the concepts being taught* to a problem-solving situation. The conceptual unit activities resume on Thursday and Friday, but the time allotments remain the same.

Week Three Schedule

Monday

Math Review—10 minutes

Process Math Review—10 minutes

Mental Math—5 minutes

Problem-Solving Task—35 minutes

Assign homework—5 minutes

- Extra Math Review practice for students who did not pass Math Review Quiz

Total minutes: 65 daily

Tuesday (time allocations same as previous day)

Math Review

Process Math Review

Mental Math

Problem-Solving Task

Assign homework

- Extra Math Review practice for students who did not pass Math Review Quiz

Wednesday (time allocations same as previous day)

Math Review

Process Math Review

Mental Math

Problem-Solving Task

Assign homework

- Extra Math Review practice for students who did not pass Math Review Quiz

Thursday (time allocations same as previous day)

Math Review

Process Math Review

Mental Math

Conceptual unit—35 minutes

Assign homework

- Extra Math Review practice for students who did not pass Math Review Quiz

Friday

Math Review Quiz—30 minutes

Score quiz together (optional)—10 minutes

Math Review self-reflection (optional, but recommended)—
5 minutes

Conceptual unit—30 minutes

Total minutes: 60 to 75

In week four, the second-grade teacher returns to the conceptual unit and continues to follow the same schedule as in weeks one and two. Depending on the length of the unit, the teacher may choose to include one or two more Problem-Solving Tasks related to the conceptual unit focus in alternating weeks five and seven (whenever the unit extends that long).

Part 2: Frequently Asked Questions

Following are the most frequently asked questions we receive from across the country during the *Five Easy Steps to a Balanced Math Program* workshops. Because these questions are relevant and applicable to primary, upper elementary, and secondary grades, we have included this section in all three editions of *Five Easy Steps to a Balanced Math Program*.

The responses to these questions have been organized according to each of the first four steps only. Readers interested in learning more about the implementation of step 5, Common Formative Assessment, are encouraged to refer to the published works on this topic, several of which are cited in Chapter 5.

Step 1: Computational Skills (Math Review and Mental Math)

Math Review.

Q. *Do I need to do Math Review every day?*

A. The Math Review process is most successful if students complete it daily. Students need multiple opportunities to practice problems if they are to become proficient with self-diagnosis. The learning process must involve repeated reasoning and "shaping" opportunities that allow students to develop or "shape" their understanding about a particular concept or skill. Students learn by trying a skill, receiving feedback on that skill, shaping their understanding about that skill, and then trying the skill again. Typically, it takes 24 repetitions with a skill to reach 80% accuracy (Marzano, 2001, p. 67).

Part 2: Frequently Asked Questions

Q. *Is it necessary to do five problems every day?*

A. The number of problems can be adjusted according to the amount of classroom time allotted to math instruction. Five problems fit within most math instructional-minute models. It is important not to do more than five problems, because you do not want Math Review to take over your daily math program. Our experience shows that five problems allow the teacher to successfully address (and close!) the gaps in student understanding of computational skills.

Q. *Is it effective to organize math problems by type and work on only one type of problem per day?*

A. Organizing problems by type within the Math Review process and working on one type each day does not allow students the multiple opportunities they need to diagnose their misunderstandings and receive necessary feedback. As stated earlier, students need multiple opportunities to shape their understanding of a concept or skill. The *Five Easy Steps* process allows students to practice multiple skills for several days and to receive feedback on each of those skills every day, increasing the probability that students will actually understand and thus retain those skills.

Q. *Is it necessary to do the Math Review Quiz?*

A. The Math Review Quiz is essential to the Math Review process (beginning in grade 1). The Math Review Quiz gives the teacher the diagnostic information necessary to determine the effectiveness of instruction; more importantly, the quiz provides students with necessary feedback about their own degree of understanding. After practicing skills and then reflecting on those skills, students need the opportunity to check their level of understanding associated with a particular concept. The Math

Math Review is designed to review *concepts and skills that students have already received instruction in and maintain them through additional practice. It is not a process for introducing new information.*

Review Quiz also helps the teacher decide when it is time to change the particular type of problems that are being presented during Math Review.

Q. *Won't the processing of Math Review take forever?*

A. The processing methods described in this book will keep the process moving along. It does take self-discipline to keep the processing of the Math Review problems within a certain time frame, but this will become second nature after a couple of weeks.

Q. *Can I present new concepts during Math Review?*

A. Math Review is designed to *review* concepts and skills that students have already received instruction in and *maintain* them through additional practice. It is not a process for introducing new information. If Math Review is used to present formal instruction of new concepts, the timing structure presented in the book will not work.

Q. *What do I do with students who finish quickly?*

A. An effective means of differentiating Math Review is to present a daily bonus problem available to all students who finish the regular material early. This bonus problem should challenge students who feel successful with the skills presented in Math Review. Also, students who finish early are quite effective at, and greatly enjoy, providing peer assistance to other students.

Q. *Is it effective to make up all of the Math Review problems for the entire year at the beginning of the year?*

A. The Math Review process is specifically designed to help the students currently in your classroom. Also, it is a diagnostic process that the teacher uses to modify and adjust instruction to fit the needs of those students. Math Review is not intended to be a "covering the curriculum" process; it is one that should naturally unfold as students work to improve their understanding of essential mathematical skills and concepts. Therefore, it is better to create the Math Review problems as the year progresses to reflect the specific and changing instructional needs of your students.

> *It is better to create the Math Review problems as the year progresses to reflect the specific and changing instructional needs of your students.*

Q. *Could grade-level teachers rotate the responsibility for writing the Math Review problems for the entire grade level?*

A. It is effective for grade-level teams of teachers to decide together on the skills and concepts to be emphasized at their particular grade level, but sharing the writing of Math Review problems is not recommended because the problems should match the instructional needs of each teacher's students.

Q. *How does Math Review fit with commercially produced math programs that include a spiral review?*

A. Commercially produced programs can be used as a resource for sample Math Review problems, but such programs often do not precisely fit the needs of your current students. The premise for conducting a spiral review is valid: if students practice a skill periodically over time, they will remember and be successful with that skill. Commercially produced programs usually do not include a process through which students can determine why they do not understand a particular skill or concept. Because the Math Review process emphasizes error analysis, teachers are better able to diagnose student learning needs and adjust instruction accordingly than they can when using a commercially produced program that requires them to adhere to a set pacing schedule with prescribed problems. Because students have regular opportunities to self-diagnose and identify their own particular misunderstandings during Math Review, they develop and retain correct mathematical understandings.

Q. *Should I collect and look through the Math Review papers daily?*

A. Daily collection and perusal of the Math Review papers provides the teacher with valuable diagnostic information about student understanding and student misconceptions. If classroom teachers incorporate the reflective part of the Math Review process, they will receive valuable information about student errors that they can then use to differentiate instruction.

Q. *I really don't have time to include the reflective piece, so is it okay to leave it out?*

A. The reflective piece helps students pinpoint their errors and determine why they do not understand a given skill or concept. It also encourages students to become responsible for their own learning, by involving them in the instructional process. Instead of students saying, "I got the wrong answer" or "I'm bad at math," self-reflection—based on error analysis—focuses students on what they *do* understand and reveals the particular part of a concept or skill that they do not yet understand.

Mental Math.

Q. *Do I have to make up the Mental Math problems myself?*

A. Grade-level teams of teachers can make up Mental Math problems together. Also, there are commercially produced teacher support materials that have examples of Mental Math activities. Certain textbook series provide resources for Mental Math problems. Our recommendation is that you first try making up a few problems with a grade-level peer by referencing the sample Mental Math problems provided in this book and then practice creating them on your own. Before you know it, you will be quite comfortable with the process. You might even find it to be fun!

Q. *I seem to skip the Mental Math activity. Do you have any suggestions that will help me to do it on a regular basis?*

A. Regularity of practice is very important. Students need to know that it is going to happen. Mental Math is the type of activity that can be done at any time during the day. We recommend that it be done after Math Review, but there is no reason not to do it at the end of a class period, before going to lunch or recess, or before leaving for the day. Often teachers report that they are unable to do it immediately after the processing of the Math Review problems and so they schedule it whenever they can. Teachers from all over the country have confirmed what we found in our own classroom experience using Mental Math: students LOVE it and will remind you if you forget to include it!

Q. *What is the point of having a theme for Mental Math?*

A. A theme in Mental Math gives students repeated practice with patterns within the number system. A theme also provides the teacher with a method of emphasizing essential math concepts for the grade level. A good strategy is to ask students if they recognize the theme of the Mental Math problem presented.

Q. *Should I quiz students on Mental Math or give a grade for this activity?*

A. No. Mental Math is designed to be quick, informal, and fun. It is intended to be a tool for practice and development of number sense, not a tool for assessment. Mental Math provides students with an opportunity to explore different strategies involving numbers and to hear other students' strategies.

Q. *Are students capable of making up good problems?*

A. Students are very capable of making up good Mental Math problems. However, require them to make up the problem the night before they want to present it to the class, so that they (and you) have an opportunity to check its accuracy and practice saying the problem at an effective speed. Another effective technique is to distribute index cards to students who wish to present a Mental Math problem to the class. The student copies his or her problem on the card, writes his or her name on it, and submits the card to the teacher. Each day the teacher draws one of the submitted cards and that student then presents his or her problem to the class.

Allowing students to make up and present Mental Math problems is an excellent practice. Teachers gain valuable insights as to what their students understand and do not understand with regard to number sense.

Q. *How can I get all students to participate in Mental Math? A few of my students just sit there while the other students are engaged in solving the given problem.*

A. The key is to create enough success and enthusiasm for Mental Math so that everyone wants to join in. Students who initially feel uncomfortable with the process need to experience success immediately so that they are motivated to try. Demonstrating a fun and enthusiastic attitude toward the activity can bring along the most reluctant of students.

Q. *How can I help my special-needs students become more successful with Mental Math? They have difficulty doing the problems in their heads at the same pace as the rest of the class, and often give up early or don't even try.*

A. To help these students succeed, allow them to use manipulatives or write down the answers incrementally as you progress through the Mental Math string of numbers and operations. Repeating the problem allows students who need assistance a second chance to arrive at the correct answer. Modeling this process with easier problems in the beginning will help support their ability to solve the problems independently. To help all students become successful, make whatever modifications you deem appropriate.

Q. *How do I determine the themes for Mental Math?*

A. The themes for Mental Math should be based on:

- Essential math standards or math Power Standards for the grade level

- Common student misunderstandings observed across the grade level

- Patterns within the number system

- General-knowledge information that students at the grade level should have

Mental Math themes can also focus on the development of and practice with basic math facts as appropriate for the particular grade level.

> *Mental Math activities are directly linked to the concept of determining a reasonable answer— an essential skill for success in mathematics.*

Q. *I'm not used to doing math in my head. How can I improve my own ability?*

A. Teachers—as well as students—will find that the more they do Mental Math, the more successful they become with it. Each time they practice, they are becoming more and more aware of number patterns and developing their own number sense. Our brains are amazing calculators if given the chance to prove it!

Q. *Mental Math seems fun, but how is it connected to being a successful math student?*

A. Mental Math activities allow students to develop effective strategies to use with number operations that they feel comfortable with and that are accurate and reliable for them. Mental Math activities are directly linked to the concept of determining a reasonable answer—an essential skill for success in mathematics. The Mental Math process also helps students become more effective test-takers. When students learn, through daily practice, the strategies of determining a reasonable answer and eliminating incorrect answer choices, they have gained a valuable skill.

Step 2: Problem Solving

Q. *I don't have time in my math program to do problem solving the way you recommend. Why is it valuable?*

A. Problem solving, as described in step 2, allows students the opportunity to apply the mathematics they have been learning. It emphasizes mathematical reasoning and the verbal and written explanation of student thinking—skills that are essential for success not only in school and on high-stakes state tests, but in life as well. Problem solving gives students opportunities to discuss mathematics with their peers and to have their mathematical thinking validated. Discussion and peer interaction are key components of learning mathematics effectively. The time this process takes is a tremendous investment in terms of the results gained.

Q. *What do I do about students who quickly get the answer in their heads but then can't explain their thinking?*

A. Providing both teacher and student models of mathematical explanations is very helpful for students who have a difficult time explaining their math processes. These students also benefit from multiple opportunities to revise their explanations. It is important to emphasize verification or proof of answers. Teachers who value reasoning, explanation, and verification as much as they do the correct answer will greatly help the student who says, "The answer just popped into my head." Such students will become successful at communicating *how* they determined their answers.

Q. *I have always disliked word problems. How can I help my students do problem solving when I myself am not very good at it?*

A. Even if you believe that you are not a "math person," it is important to develop the attitude that you can be successful with problem solving. An effective way to begin is to select problems with grade-level colleagues and solve the problems together before assigning the problems to your students. After solving the problems with your peers, solve the problem again, making sure you understand the mathematics presented in the problem. It is very important to be patient with yourself during this process. What you will find as you do the problems with students is that you are gaining insights from the students' reasoning. You will find that you are more of a math person than you thought!

Q. *My students resist problem solving. What do I do?*

A. Start with easy problems and help students experience immediate success. It is essential that you convince students that they are capable of doing problem solving. Use the whole-class approach described in Chapter 2 until you feel that students are gaining confidence as problem solvers. Older students who have not been successful with problem solving in earlier grades will be very resistant to problem solving in the beginning. It is essential that they feel there is hope for success.

Q. *How do I know if the Problem-Solving Task I have selected is a good one, and where do I find good problems?*

A. The most important criterion in selecting a Problem-Solving Task is that it matches the current math unit topic and that classroom instruction supports it. Students should not be asked to do a task that requires mathematics in which they have not received instruction. Determine whether the problem allows application of the mathematical ideas presented in the current instructional unit of study.

Other important criteria are that the problem be:

- At an appropriate difficulty level for students
- Accessible to all students
- Relevant, engaging, and challenging
- Approachable by various ways and methods of solution

Other guidelines for selecting worthwhile problems are listed in Chapter 2. The last of these is the one we believe to be most important: that the *teacher* fully understand the mathematics in the problem, so that he or she can better facilitate student understanding. The real test of quality for a problem is whether it works for students and engages them in the process.

Many Websites for problem solving are available on the Internet, and educational publishers produce problem-solving components in their math text series. An effective way to create a grade-level collection of problems is to have all teachers in a grade level try problems in their own classrooms and share those problems with one another. In this way, each teacher will begin compiling a folder of problems that have been tried in the classroom and that match grade-level standards and particular topics of conceptual units.

Q. *How do I give a grade based on the problem-solving rubric?*

A. The main purpose of a problem-solving rubric is to provide feedback to students on their problem-solving ability, so that they have the opportunity to note where they are doing well and where they need to improve. A rubric should be designed to provide criteria for an overall performance level, not a percentage or point value. When giving a grade for problem solving within a traditional grading system, be careful that the point value, percentage score, or letter grade given reflects what is most important in students' performance: their understanding of the *mathematics*, not the criteria that have nothing to do with the actual mathematics (i.e., following directions, effort, language conventions, and so on).

Q. *Which type of rubric works best for the problem-solving
activity?*

A. Either a holistic or an analytic rubric works fine for problem
solving. An analytic rubric provides teachers and students with
specific feedback relative to each major component within the
rubric (e.g., mathematical process, strategies, vocabulary, and so
on). The drawback of using an analytic rubric is that it may be
too complicated to use or confusing to students. When using an
analytic rubric in a traditional grading system, the letter grade
or percentage derived from it can be very misleading in terms
of determining student understanding of the mathematics in
the problem. If a point system is attached to the criteria in
an analytic rubric, students can gather points for items that do
not relate to the mathematics and thus misleadingly inflate
the student's overall performance.

We recommend using a holistic rubric designed for use with
every Problem-Solving Task, such as the one presented in
Chapter 2. Not only is it easier to use, but it also keeps both
students and teachers sharply focused on the evidence of
student understanding and on the mathematics used to solve
the problem.

Step 3: Conceptual Understanding

Q. *I'm used to using a textbook for math instruction. How can
I adjust to the conceptual unit approach?*

A. A textbook should be a resource to help you teach the standards
at your grade level. If you are used to following a textbook as
your guide for instruction, an easy way to transition to a conceptual unit approach is to start by examining your grade-level

standards and identifying which standards are presented effectively by the textbook and which are not. For standards that are not effectively presented in the textbook, collaborate with other grade-level teachers and design a unit of study using the guidelines presented in Chapter 3. Another suggestion is to design just one conceptual unit per quarter when first implementing the *Five Easy Steps* program; then build to two per quarter the next year; and so on.

Typically, teachers using the Five Easy Steps *program develop approximately six conceptual units of instruction during the course of a school year.*

Q. *How many Conceptual Understanding Units should I teach each year?*

A. The number of units you develop and teach depends on your particular grade level and how effectively your math standards can be grouped around a common topic. All math is interrelated, but for the sake of instruction you want to be able to determine four or five essential mathematical understandings for one unit of study. Typically, teachers using the *Five Easy Steps* program develop approximately six conceptual units of instruction during the course of a school year.

Q. *How can I teach Conceptual Understanding Units of instruction and still cover all the standards for my grade level? There is not enough time to have students fully understand what they are doing. I have to keep moving, or I will fall behind the pace established by my district. Why should I consider this approach?*

A. The conceptual unit approach to teaching mathematics is based on teaching for understanding, not on covering material. There is no educational support for the idea that just covering learning objectives helps students learn that information. Therefore, the choice each of us has to make is this: Do I help my students *understand* mathematics, or do I move on whether they know it or not? Learning mathematics is a building process. If a strong foundation of understanding is not established, teachers can cover, cover, cover all they want, and students will just get further and further behind. That is why we strongly endorse the practice of identifying math Power Standards—those *prioritized* standards that all students need for success each year in school, in life, and on all high-stakes assessments.

Q. *How does the conceptual unit approach help test scores?*

A. Helping students deeply understand essential concepts and skills they are expected to know and be able to do will always help test scores. The conceptual unit approach is intentionally designed to develop student understanding around essential grade-level math standards (Power Standards). Following the process outlined in Chapter 3 will help teachers design and teach conceptual units matched to grade-level math expectations. This is a powerful practice that is sure to prepare students for success, not only on state assessments, but also in understanding and applying math in succeeding years of school and throughout their lives.

Q. *Why should students understand mathematics conceptually? I learned math procedurally, and I did fine. I made it through college by memorizing procedures.*

A. Learning math procedurally means memorizing a series of steps to get an answer. Procedural mathematics is very answer-focused, and not at all meaning-based. Conceptual instruction allows students to make sense of mathematics, to see the patterns and connections within mathematics, while learning a concept and then the procedure attached to that concept.

A series of memorized steps is easily forgotten and easily mixed up with other memorized steps.

Math textbooks in this country have become longer and longer because each year students have to review what they supposedly learned in the preceding grade. Furthermore, teaching mathematics without attached meaning has become an issue of equity in the United States. Many students are not successful in math because math never made sense to them. It has even become acceptable in our culture to say, "I'm not a math person." Continuing this type of instructional approach and mindset prevents many students from achieving their full potential as mathematically powerful students.

Q. *How long should a Conceptual Understanding Unit last?*

A. A conceptual unit will usually last a few weeks, as described in Chapter 3. However, the actual length of your unit will depend on the amount of time you dedicate to actual math instruction on a daily basis. The number of standards related to a particular topic usually determines the duration of the unit.

Q. *I noticed in the recommended schedule for my specific grade level that you assign homework, but no time was allocated for the processing of that homework the next day. When do you go over homework?*

A. Assigned homework should relate to the instruction that students are receiving within the conceptual unit. Effective homework gives students the opportunity to practice the skills or concepts that they are learning in school. Such homework can be quickly reviewed at the beginning of the conceptual unit instruction portion of the math period.

Using each of the five steps of this model will help all students become successful in mathematics, even within the constraints of a district pacing chart.

Q. *My district has a pacing chart for instruction in math, and we are all expected to follow it. How does the conceptual unit approach fit with this situation?*

A. Pacing charts can make teaching for understanding a real challenge. Douglas B. Reeves, nationally recognized expert on standards, assessment, and accountability, often says this in his keynote addresses regarding the use of pacing charts:

> *There is not a single state standard that requires students to "do algebra quickly." Rather, the standards require them to do algebra, and every other subject, proficiently. This emphasis on proficiency explicitly rejects speed as a criterion for evaluation, unless (as in keyboarding, for example) speed is inherent in proficiency. In the vast majority of performances in school as well as the world of work, the most effective model is not one of hasty, slipshod work. It is a process of submitting work, getting feedback on the work, and improving the work. This is what great leaders and teachers do in all subjects and in all walks of life.*

The reasoning that all students will learn a math concept by a certain date is a bit dumbfounding. However, if teachers follow the process outlined in Chapter 3, they can still effectively use standards to determine what is essential to teach for student understanding. It all comes down to maintaining a sharp focus on what is truly critical for students to know and be able to do mathematically. Using each of the five steps of this model will help all students become successful in mathematics, even within the constraints of a district pacing chart. Teachers should trust their professional judgment and modify or adjust any preset instructional pace so as to meet the learning needs of their students. They must also consider the negative effects on student learning and retention if they do not.

Q. *How can I teach for understanding if I don't understand the mathematics myself?*

A. The steps outlined in this book are designed primarily to help your students become successful at mathematics, but they are also designed to help the classroom teacher feel more confident about teaching for understanding. Learning any new professional practice can be a bit uncomfortable, but allow yourself time to follow the guidelines in the book. You will find that your attitude toward and confidence with math will improve. You will find that you can indeed understand mathematics, and that you can do a more effective job of teaching it than you might have thought!

Q. *I know that other countries teach math differently than we do in the United States and get very good results. How do other countries develop units of study in mathematics?*

A. Asian countries, for example, use a method called "Lesson Study" to develop their curricula in mathematics. The process is highly collaborative. Teachers design lessons together, watch each other teach those lessons, and then revise the lessons based on professional feedback. Asian teachers also use the knowledge package idea (described in Chapter 3) to determine all the components of math that connect to the concept they will be teaching in a conceptual unit of instruction. This results in effective lessons that are grouped into units of study and shared with all who teach that grade level.

Step 4: Mastery of Math Facts

Q: *We do a "Mad Minute" worksheet every day to start the math
period. Won't that help my students memorize their facts?*

A. Timing students on their math facts does not teach them
anything except to be nervous! The "Mad Minute" approach
does not allow students to develop effective strategies for fact
retrieval. It does not assist development of pattern knowledge,
nor does it provide them with any information about the
number system. Timing is part of assessment, not instruction.
For further guidelines and information on this important
question, please refer to Chapter 4.

Q. *Why do so many students not remember their math facts?
I learned math facts from the drill-and-kill method. Why
doesn't that work for my students?*

A. Actually, you most likely did not learn your facts from the drill-
and-kill method; you remembered the facts because you were
able to find a pattern or an association that allowed you to
recall the facts when necessary. Students today do not remember
math facts because of *the way* they are taught those facts.
Most likely, they are not being intentionally led to discover the
underlying concepts for learning math facts, which become
evident when teachers emphasize the particular math-facts
patterns appropriate for each grade level; rather, they are just
expected to memorize the facts. Drill is effective only when it
is drill of efficient strategies that the student has developed
for fact retrieval. Math-fact retrieval is highly dependent on the
development of strong number sense. Please refer to Chapter 1,
in the sections related to Math Review, for ideas that will help
students develop strong number sense, and also consult Chapter
4 for math-fact strategies.

Part 2: Frequently Asked Questions

Q. *Don't students have to prove that they know their math facts within a time constraint? Also, if I don't time my students, won't that affect their standardized test scores?*

A. One of the most frequent and problematic questions we hearfrom math teachers concerns students learning their math facts within timed-testing conditions. Educators ask, "To develop automaticity with regard to their math facts, don't

students have to be timed? Isn't speed essential?"

Automatic retrieval of math facts comes when students developeffective strategies for retrieval based on their knowledge of the number system. Practice with strategies that are effective and reliable for each student is the key to automatic retrieval.

Mental Math activities are excellent for helping students develop strong number sense. Timing has nothing to do with students becoming proficient with math facts. Unfortunately,timing has led many students to decide that they are "bad at math." Timed math-fact recall must not continue to be the central issue: student *understanding* and *effective practice* of math facts are what we must emphasize.

Q. *What about students who count on their fingers to get the answer to a basic math fact?*

A. Students who are still counting on their fingers after first or second grade are letting the teacher know that they have not developed the idea of quantity, and that they have very limited number sense. The issue is not the use of their fingers, but that these students are *counting every thing individually, as opposed to considering patterns* within the number system. The infor- mation in this book about Math Review, Mental Math, and mathfacts offers effective ways to help students who still need to develop their number sense.

> *Automatic retrieval of math facts comes when students develop effective strategies for retrieval based on their knowledgeof the number system.*

Q. *Should math-fact development be separate from the regular math program?*

A. Math-fact development should be *embedded* in daily math instruction. The Math Review and Mental Math processes will help you incorporate math-fact development within the regular math program.

Q. *How can parents play a part in their children's math-fact development?*

A. Parents can help their children develop number sense outside of school. Parents can ask their children to count by a given number, find combinations that make 5 and 10, talk about numbers, point out numbers when shopping or traveling, read books about numbers, and develop a positive attitude toward mathematics. They can play card and board games involving numbers with their children. Parents can engage children in measurement tasks at home and practice computing math problems mentally while driving to practices or appointments.

Closing Thoughts

We fully recognize the amount of initial thinking and preparation needed to implement a balanced math program, *because we have done this work ourselves.* Designing a conceptual unit for the first time may be challenging. The first time you present a Problem-Solving Task to your students may seem daunting. The first time you write a math rubric with colleagues or with your students may be as much of an education for you as it is for them. Once you have made each of these practices your own, though, you will be able to continuously refine that practice in the following months and years. When you can provide your students with the ingredients necessary to become mathematically powerful, we think you will agree that it was more than worth the effort.

If you have any questions that were not addressed in this or the previous chapters, or others that arise as you begin using these steps in your own classrooms, please do not hesitate to contact us. Our e-mail addresses are in the "About the Authors" section at the beginning of the book. We will be more than happy to assist you in any way we can.

Best wishes as you begin balancing your math program in *Five Easy Steps*!

CHAPTER 10

As instructional leaders, school administrators often request guidelines for overseeing the effective implementation of the Five Easy Steps *math program in their individual schools. In this final chapter, we provide several documents that school leaders can use for this purpose.*

Executive Summary

This first document is an executive summary of the balanced math program. It provides an overview and a brief description of each of the steps. Administrators may duplicate this document to share and discuss with central office administrators, parents, and faculty.

Five Easy Steps to a Balanced Math Program
An Overview for Leaders and Leadership Teams
By Larry Ainsworth and Jan Christinson

Each step in the *Five Easy Steps to a Balanced Math Program* focuses on a different but interdependent practice that will help all students in grades K–12 become, in time, mathematically powerful. To realize the best results, the authors recommend that teachers follow the guidelines for effective implementation presented in the three books (primary, upper elementary, and secondary editions) and in the handout received at the *Five Easy Steps* workshop. Also, note that there is a suggested time frame in each of these resources that teachers can follow to make the steps manageable during a math lesson that takes approximately one hour.

Step 1: Computational Skills (Math Review and Mental Math). Math Review and Mental Math are daily practices designed to keep students "skill sharp" with regard to math concepts and procedures they have learned in prior lessons and units of study. Math Review is especially valuable in helping students: (1) remember what they were taught days, weeks, or months earlier; (2) apply or extend that learning as they encounter new concepts and skills; and (3) carry forward what they have learned into succeeding years. Math Review also helps close the gaps for students who are performing below proficiency on grade-level math standards, by providing daily practice and review of essential concepts and skills.

Math Review and Mental Math should be conducted *daily,* as described in the resources. The power of Math Review and Mental Math lies in regular practice. Teachers should *process* selected problems with students each day, emphasizing reasonable answers and the development of effective math strategies. Math Review and Mental Math can also provide teachers with a daily opportunity to introduce and maintain key math vocabulary. An accountability quiz (the Math Review Quiz) should be given every week, or every other week at the least, to inform teacher instruction and pinpoint needed interventions or accelerations for students. Students are encouraged to self-assess their own progress, identify where they need to improve, and develop a plan to achieve that improvement.

Step 2: Problem Solving. The Problem-Solving Task Write-Up Guide templates—different ones are provided in the texts for primary, upper elementary, and secondary grades—provide a simple but effective framework within which students learn to solve multiple-step math problems. First, students use calculation and graphic representation (words, pictures, and/or numbers) to solve the given problem, and then write a description, in their own words, of the process they followed. It is recommended that students practice the problem-solving write-up process on a regular basis throughout the school year until they are able to complete it independently. Teachers should select engaging, multiple-step problems that relate to the conceptual math units being taught (particularly those aligned to the math Power Standards) so that students can *apply* the mathematics they are learning to real-life math contexts. A generic problem-solving rubric is developed by individual grade levels or grade spans (primary, upper elementary, secondary) to assess student work. As with the Math Review (account-ability) Quiz, students are encouraged to self-assess their own progress, identify where they need to improve, and develop a plan to achieve that improvement.

Step 3: Conceptual Understanding. To deepen students' conceptual understanding, it is essential that teachers deliver conceptual units of instruction based on key "unwrapped" math Power Standards aligned to end-of-unit assessment tasks. It is recommended that teachers design and teach a Conceptual Understanding Unit concerning math concepts and skills that are the most difficult for students to grasp. The recommended sequence for designing conceptual units is presented in each of the *Five Easy Steps* books. Participating teachers design a Conceptual Understanding Unit during the *Five Easy Steps* workshop. Schools are encouraged to create a "bank" of math conceptual units, with performance-based assessments, to help busy teachers work smarter, not harder.

Step 4: Mastery of Math Facts. Math-fact mastery is the responsibility of elementary schools. Students should enter middle school with their math facts learned. To achieve a systematic plan to ensure this, teachers within each elementary school— working with their administrators—first collaboratively determine which math facts are appropriate for student mastery *by the end of* each school year. They cross-reference their selections with the state standards and make whatever modifications are necessary to their grade-level assignment of facts. They then create a "math-facts map" that identifies which facts are to be mastered at each grade level, beginning with kindergarten and ending with grade 5. Lastly, a math-facts assessment schedule is developed for each grade. The grade-assigned facts and assessment schedule are then published and explained to both students and parents. A key emphasis in the *Five Easy Steps* approach to mastery of math facts is that students first learn the facts through an emphasis on discovering mathematical patterns, rather than rote drill or memorization.

Step 5: Common Formative Assessment. This final step is a grade-level math assessment *for* learning that participating teachers collaboratively design, administer, score, and analyze in order to differentiate instruction. These common formative assessments should be designed to assess *only* the math Power Standards. They are aligned to conceptual end-of-unit assessments in the classroom. Common formative assessments are typically based on a pre-/post-assessment design model and administered multiple times during the school year. Assessment items should represent different formats, including selected response, short constructed-response, and extended response. Teachers often choose to make these formats similar to those used on state assessments. This multiple-measures approach to assessment typically provides broader insights into student understanding. The teachers analyze the results of the student assessments in order to set a short-term instructional goal, and then select effective teaching strategies to achieve it. The student assessment results are used to inform and differentiate instruction so that the diverse learning needs of all students are met. When aligned to district quarterly mathassessments, end-of-course math assessments, and even state math assessments, common formative assessments provide predictive value as to how students are likely to do on those external assessments—in time for teachers to make needed modifications in instruction.

Math Leadership Team Planning Questions

Rather than assign the full responsibility for the implementation of *Five Easy Steps* to the principal or assistant principal alone, more and more schools are assembling school leadership teams comprised of the school administrator *and* grade-level or department representatives. It is their collective responsibility to oversee the effective implementation of *Five Easy Steps* in their building. This second document lists specific questions related to each of the steps to assist the school leadership team with planning.

Math Leadership Team Planning Questions

Five Easy Steps to a Balanced Math Program

Math Leadership Team Planning Questions *By*

Jan Christinson and Larry Ainsworth

Step 1: Computational Skills (Math Review and Mental Math)

- Is every classroom implementing Math Review and Mental Math?
- How consistently are both of these practices being used in each grade level or department?
- Do teachers emphasize reasonable answer and math strategies with students when they process daily Math Review problems?
- What kinds of Math Review formats are teachers using at each grade level?
- What core math vocabulary should teachers introduce and maintain at each grade level?
- Are teachers emphasizing math vocabulary in Math Review and Mental Math?
- How often are teachers administering the Math Review (accountability) Quiz?
- Who provides the problems, individual teachers or grade-level teams?
- What additional resources or training do teachers need?
- Do new teachers know how to use Math Review and Mental Math?

Step 2: Problem Solving

- What should problem solving look like at each grade level and in each course?
- Which core problem-solving strategies should all teachers be using?
- Are students learning these same core problem-solving strategies?
- Are grade-level teams selecting or creating multiple-step problems that match the Conceptual Understanding Units being taught?

- How often are grade levels administering the Problem-Solving Task Write-Up work?
- How are teachers assessing problem solving? (individual teacher rubric, grade-level rubric, grade-span rubric, district-wide rubric)
- Are students involved in self- and peer-assessment?
- Are students reflecting on their progress (where they are doing well, where they need to improve)? Are we helping students to develop improvement goals?
- What training or support do teachers need to incorporate problem solving on a regular basis?

Step 3: Conceptual Understanding

- How is the school leadership team encouraging conceptual teaching (teaching for meaning) in mathematics?
- How can we help all teachers do more conceptual teaching?
- Which of our teachers could mentor other teachers in this regard?
- Which prioritized math standards (Power Standards) should all teachers be emphasizing at each grade?
- Are teachers "unwrapping" the math Power Standards for their grades? Is this happening in each classroom?
- Are teachers determining Big Ideas and Essential Questions to guide and focus their instruction and assessments?
- What grade-level Conceptual Understanding Units are teachers designing for topics that are particularly challenging for students to learn?
- Are the conceptual units aligned with end-of-unit assessments and accompanying rubrics or scoring guides?
- Are we creating a bank of grade-level conceptual units that all teachers can contribute to and use?

Step 4: Mastery of Math Facts

- Does the school have a plan that vertically maps the math facts in all four basic operations across the K–5 grades? Does this plan reflect or clarify the math facts listed in the state standards?

Math Leadership Team Planning Questions

- Is a math-facts assessment schedule in place at each grade?
- Do parents and students understand the school-wide math-facts plan and grade-specific assessment schedule?
- What help do teachers need to teach math facts through patterns, as opposed to drill and rote memorization only?
- What resources do teachers need to teach and assess their students' grasp of grade-level math facts?

Step 5: Common Formative Math Assessments

- Which grades are administering common math assessments *for* learning? How often?
- Are these assessments aligned to the math Power Standards?
- Are these assessments aligned to the district quarterly math assessments?
- Are grade levels collaboratively designing and scoring these assessments?
- Do these assessments include more than one format (selected response, short-constructed response, extended response)?
- Are grade levels analyzing the student data in grade-level or department Data Teams?
- Are assessment results being used to differentiate instruction (intervening for students at risk and accelerating for proficient and advanced students)?

6. Time Line

- Which of the *Five Easy Steps* will be our priority for school-wide implementation this year? Next year? The year after that?
- What is our projected date for complete school-wide implementation of all five steps?
- Have we prioritized our action plans to accomplish the most important tasks first?

Alignment Diagram

Educators and leaders are rightfully demanding to know how any new initiative or practice fits into the larger picture of standards, assessment, and accountability. The following diagram (introduced and explained in Chapter 5) represents the integration and inter-dependency of these practices. For a detailed description of this diagram and how each practice is closely and deliberately aligned with the others, please refer to *Common Formative Assessments: How to Connect Standards-Based Instruction and Assessment* (Ainsworth & Viegut, 2006). This diagram represents the interface of these practices with the *Five Easy Steps to a Balanced Math Program.*

Alignment Diagram

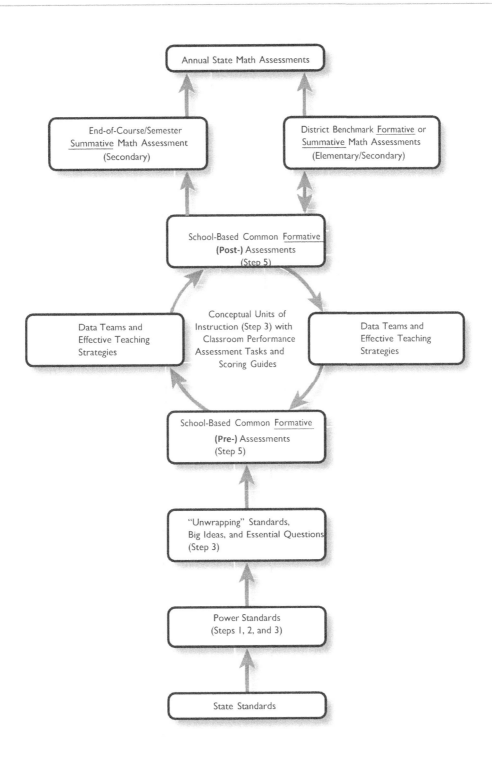

Adapted from *Common Formative Assessments: How to Connect Standards-Based Instruction and Assessment* (Ainsworth & Viegut, Corwin Press, 2006).

A Framework for Implementation

This final document provides a three-column template that school leaders or school leadership teams can use as a planning blueprint for effective implementation of each of the *Five Easy Steps*. The authors would like to acknowledge and thank Laura Besser of The Leadership and Learning Center for developing this template, into which we inserted the content relevant to *Five Easy Steps*.

The descriptions in the "Desired State" column represent key indicators of full implementation that leaders should expect to see when the steps are fully implemented in individual classrooms and grade levels. Readers are encouraged to add other indicators of their choice.

To use this planning blueprint effectively, we recommend that the school leadership team conduct an honest assessment of the school's current reality with regard to each of the five steps. The team can then record those indicators in the "Current State" column.

When the first column is completed, record in the middle column the "Action Steps" that your leadership team and faculty members will need to take to achieve the indicators in the "Desired State" column. As part of this last step, it may be necessary first to identify the obstacles (perceived or real) standing in the way of effective implementation of each action step. During the process of identifying those obstacles, the needed action steps may become readily apparent.

A Framework for Implementation

Once this is finished, draft a preliminary time frame for the first year of implementation. When ready, repeat the process for the second and third years of implementation. These timelines should remain flexible and be adjusted as the school moves through the process. However, adhering to a short- and long-term schedule, as much as possible, will help the school stay on track toward achieving the "Desired State" goals.

Two blank, full-size versions of the planning template appear in the "Reproducibles" section at the end of this book.

It is our hope that these documents, individually and collectively, will assist leaders and leadership teams in implementing and sustaining *Five Easy Steps to a Balanced Math Program*. Again, please contact the authors at the e-mail addresses provided in the "About the Authors" section at the beginning of this book should you have further questions.

A Framework for Implementing
Five Easy Steps to a Balanced Math Program

What do math instruction and assessment *currently* look like in our school? (Sample responses)

Math Instruction	Math Assessment
• Varied approaches and styles • Mainly traditional approach • Textbook-driven • More lecture, less student involvement • Teacher-centered • Learning targets not always clear • Chapter-based vs. standards-based • Inch-deep, mile-wide coverage • Differentiation, but not enough to meet wide diversity of student needs • Monitoring/adjustment of instruction • Practice worksheets • Some peer tutoring • Some cooperative learning	• More summative than formative • Chapter and unit tests • District benchmark "dipstick" quarterly math assessments aligned to the state test • End-of-course assessments at secondary level • Certain schools are beginning to use common math assessments • Assessment not used to drive instruction

A Framework for Implementation

Key for *Five Easy Steps* Terms

CFA Common Formative Assessment   **MR** Math Review

FES Five Easy Steps   **PS** Power Standards

MM Mental Math   **PST** Problem-Solving Task

STEP 1: Computational Skills (Math Review and Mental Math)

Current State	Action Steps	Desired State
•	•	• All grades using MR and MM daily
•	•	• Teacher-designed problems based on current needs of students
•	•	• Teachers emphasize reasonable answer and math strategies with students during processing of MR problems
•	•	• Math Review Quiz given weekly or biweekly
•	•	• Appropriate MR formats used at each grade level
•	•	• Math vocabulary incorporated into MR and MM
•	•	
•	•	

Step 2: Problem Solving

Current State	Action Steps	Desired State
•	•	• Core problem-solving strategies identified and used by all teachers
•	•	• Core problem-solving strategies taught to students
•	•	• Grade-level teams select or create multistep PSTs that match Conceptual Understanding Units
•	•	• Grade levels administer a PST at least twice a month
•	•	• Problem solving assessed with generic rubric applicable to all PSTs
•	•	• Students involved in self- and peer-assessment
•	•	• Students reflect on their progress (where they are doing well, where they need to improve) and develop goal/plan for improvement
•	•	• Ongoing support for teachers identified and provided as needed
•	•	

Step 3: Conceptual Understanding

Current State	Action Steps	Desired State
•	•	• Conceptual teaching taking place at every grade level
•	•	• Grade-level mentor teachers assist colleagues with conceptual teaching as needed
•	•	• Core math standards (PS) identified and emphasized in conceptual units of instruction
•	•	• Math standards "unwrapped" to pinpoint key concepts and skills
•	•	• Big Ideas and Essential Questions used to focus instruction and assessment
•	•	• Math vocabulary identified and emphasized at each grade level
•	•	• Grade-level conceptual units, including aligned end-of-unit assessments, used to teach students "unwrapped" math PS concepts and skills
•	•	• School and/or district bank of grade-level math conceptual units established, for all teachers to use and contribute to
•	•	

Step 4: Mastery of Math Facts

Current State	Action Steps	Desired State
•	•	• School plan in place that vertically maps all math facts in the four basic operations across grades K–5
•	•	• School plan reflects or clarifies the math facts listed in state standards
•	•	• Math-facts assessment schedule in place at each grade
•	•	• Parents and students understand school-wide plan and grade-specific assessment schedule
•	•	• Math facts taught through patterns, rather than memorization only
•	•	• Necessary resources are available for teaching and assessing students' mastery of grade-level math facts
•	•	
•	•	
•	•	

Step 5: Common Formative Assessment

Current State	Action Steps	Desired State
•	•	• Grade levels administer collaboratively designed, short-cycle math assessments *for* learning
•	•	• CFAs aligned to math PS and classroom end-of-unit assessments
•	•	• Assessments aligned to district quarterly math assessments
•	•	• CFAs include more than one type of format (selected response, short-constructed response, extended response)
•	•	• Grade levels collaboratively score math CFAs
•	•	• Grade levels analyze student data in grade-level or department Data Teams
•	•	• Assessment results used to differentiate instruction (interventions for students at risk and accelerations for proficient and advanced students)
•	•	
•	•	
•	•	

Five Easy Steps Prioritized Time Frame for Implementation

Time Frame—Year 1	What We Want to Have in Place
September (list school year)	•
October	•
November	•
December	•
January	•
February	•
March	•
April	•
May	•
June	•
Summer	•

Five Easy Steps Prioritized Time Frame for Implementation *(Continued)*

Time Frame—Year 2	What We Want to Have in Place
August	•
September (list school year)	•
October	•
November	•
December	•
January	•
February	•
March	•
April	•
May	•
Summer	•

(continues)

Five Easy Steps Prioritized Time Frame for Implementation *(Continued)*

Time Frame—Year 3	What We Want to Have in Place
August	•
September (list school year)	•
October	•
November	•
December	•
January	•
February	•
March	•
April	•
May	•
Summer	•

Reproducibles

In this section we have included reproducible versions of templates and charts that appear within the chapters. The reader has permission to duplicate these for instructional use only.

They are presented in the following sequence:

Step 1: Computational Skills (Math Review and Mental Math). There are three templates that can be used for a given week of Math Review and Mental Math. The third template is for the teacher to copy and use as a visual display each day.

Step 2: Problem Solving. We have provided a sample Problem-Solving Task Write-Up Guide for primary grades and a recommended problem-solving rubric. Also included is a summary of problem-solving steps written specifically for students in primary grades.

Step 3: Conceptual Understanding. Included here is the template used to design a conceptual unit, with all the components described in Chapter 3 and illustrated with grade-specific examples in Chapters 6, 7, and 8.

Step 4: Mastery of Math Facts. Primary-grade teachers typically design their own templates and assessments for math facts, so we have not included any examples here. However, we do provide a summary of patterns used to teach math facts, with grade-specific listings for guidance through grade 5 and notes for middle school. Suggestions for practice are listed thereafter, to be used as appropriate for your grade and your particular students' needs.

Step 5: Common Formative Assessment. The *Five Easy Steps* Balanced Math Alignment Diagram that appears in Chapter 5 is reproduced here as a "big picture" that shows the interrelationships between the *Five Easy Steps* framework and other powerful practices related to standards, assessment, and accountability.

We have also included, at the end of this section, two copies of the template that appears in Chapter 10, "A Framework for Implementing *Five Easy Steps to a Balanced Math Program*." Educators and leaders can use this template to plan for the successful implementation of each of the five steps over three successive years.

Daily Math Review

Name _____

Monday

Number Sense   Addition   Subtraction

Patterns   Measurement   Bonus

Mental Math   1._____   2._____   3. _____

Tuesday

Number Sense   Addition   Subtraction

Patterns   Measurement   Bonus

Mental Math   1._____   2._____   3. _____

Daily Math Review

Name _____

Wednesday

| Number Sense | Addition | Subtraction |

| Patterns | Measurement | Bonus |

Mental Math   1._____   2._____   3. _____

Thursday

| Number Sense | Addition | Subtraction |

| Patterns | Measurement | Bonus |

Mental Math   1._____   2._____   3. _____

Five Easy Steps to a Balanced Math Program for Primary Grades

Daily Math Review Visual Display

Name _____

Number Sense	Addition	Subtraction

Patterns	Measurement	Bonus

Mental Math

1._____ 2._____ 3. _____

Problem-Solving Task Write-Up Guide: Primary

Directions:

1. Write your name on a piece of paper.

2. Solve the problem using words, pictures, and/or numbers.

3. Number each step as you work to solve the problem.

4. Write a number sentence to match your problem.

5. Write your answer in a sentence under your solution.

6. Now write a short paragraph that explains, step by step, how you solved the problem.

7. Use math vocabulary.

8. Use this write-up guide to help you write your paragraph:

Data Sheet:

Solve the problem using words, pictures, and/or numbers.

Write-Up:

First I_____. Next I _____

_____ . Then I_____.

After that I_____.

Finally, I_____.

Five Easy Steps to a Balanced Math Program for Primary Grades

Problem-Solving Scoring Guide: Primary

Exemplary:

- ❑ All "Proficient" criteria *plus:*
- ❑ Written work explains, step by step, the process used to solve the problem

Proficient:

- ❑ Correct answer
- ❑ Solves problem on Data Sheet with words, pictures, and/or numbers
- ❑ Includes number sentence that matches problem
- ❑ Follows all Problem-Solving Guide directions to complete write-up

Progressing:

- ❑ Meets 3 of the "Proficient" criteria

Beginning:

- ❑ Meets fewer than 3 of the "Proficient" criteria
- ❑ Task to be repeated after remediation

Self-Evaluation _____

I think my score is a_____because _____

_____

Teacher's Evaluation_____because _____

_____

Note: Proficiency must address the mathematics.

Students have ongoing opportunities to reflect upon and revise their work with feedback using the scoring guide.

Problem-Solving Steps for Primary Students

Get Ready to Solve the Problem.

1. Read the problem first.

2. Underline or circle the important facts and key words.

3. What are you supposed to find out?

4. Are there any "tricky" parts to the problem?

5. What math vocabulary words are in the problem?

6. Which math strategies will you use?

7. Do you need manipulatives or other math tools to help you?

Solve the Problem.

1. Solve the problem using words, pictures, and/or numbers.

2. Number each of your problem-solving steps (1, 2, 3, . . .) on your Data Sheet.

3. Write a number sentence to show how you solved the problem.

4. Write your answer in a word sentence after you complete your steps.

5. Check your work to see if it makes sense.

Write How You Solved the Problem.

1. Find the first math step you did on your Data Sheet (the step labeled #1).

2. Complete the sentence starter, "First I . . . ," writing what you did first. (This should *not* be: "First I read the problem.")

3. Find the second math step you did on your Data Sheet (the step labeled #2).

4. Complete the sentence starter, "Next I . . . ," writing what you did second.

5. ontinue this way until you have written a sentence for each of the other numbered math steps. Use other transition words (*next, then, after that, finally*) to help you.

6. Use math vocabulary in as many sentences as you can.

7. Check each sentence to make sure it describes a *math step*.

8. Check to make sure each sentence makes sense.

Want a Bonus Challenge?

1. Can you add the word *because* after each math step you write and then explain why you did that step?

2. Can you include other math vocabulary words to help explain how you solved the problem?

3. Can you solve the problem in more than one way?

4. Can you find someone who solved it differently than you did?

5. Can you change the problem to make it more challenging?

6. Can you solve your own challenging problem?

7. Can you find someone else who will try to solve your problem?

Five Easy Steps to a Balanced Math Program

Step 3

Conceptual Understanding Unit Design Template

Grade Level: _____

Conceptual Unit Focus: _____

Standards and Indicators Matched to Unit Focus: _____

"Unwrapped" Concepts:

"Unwrapped" Skills:
———

Topics or Context: (Specific lessons, textbook pages, learning activities teachers will use during unit)

Conceptual Understanding Unit Design Template *(Continued)*

Knowledge Package Cluster:

Big Ideas:

_____

_____

_____

_____

_____

Essential Questions:

_____

_____

_____

_____

End-of-Unit Assessment:

Conceptual Understanding Unit Design Template *(Continued)*

Scoring Guide

Exemplary:

❑ All "Proficient" criteria *plus*:

❑ _____

❑ _____

❑ _____

Proficient:

❑ _____

❑ _____

❑ _____

❑ _____

Progressing:

❑ _____

❑ _____

❑ _____

❑ _____

Beginning:

❑ _____

❑ _____

Self-Evaluation _____

Teacher's Evaluation _____

Comments _____

_____

_____

(continues)

Conceptual Understanding Unit Design Template *(Continued)*

Lessons and Activities Students Need to Understand
"Unwrapped" Concepts, Skills, and Big Ideas:

_____

_____

_____

_____

_____

_____

_____

_____

_____

_____

_____

_____

_____

_____

_____

_____

_____

_____

Conceptual Understanding Unit Design Template *(Continued)*

Teacher Reflections:

1. *What worked? What didn't?* _____

_____

_____

_____

_____

2. *What will I do differently next time?*

_____

_____

_____

_____

3. *What student work samples do I have?*

_____

_____

_____

_____

4. *What suggestions can I provide for other teachers who may use this assessment?*

_____

_____

_____

_____

Step 4: Mastery of Math Facts
Using Patterns: A K-5 Summary

Patterns that will help K-2 students learn math facts and develop improved number sense include:
- One more than and two more than a number (8 + 1, 8 + 2, and so on)
- Facts with zero (0 + 2, 0 + 3, and so on)
- Doubles (2 + 2, 5 + 5, 9 + 9, and so on)
- Facts that make five (3 + 2, 2 + 3, and so on)
- Facts that make ten (7 + 3, 2 + 8, and so on)
- Part-part-whole relationships (fact-family groups)
- Addition and subtraction as inverse operations

Patterns by Grade

A grade-specific summary of the patterns used to teach students math facts follows:

Kindergarten:
- The quantity of a number
- How to correctly say a number
- One more than a number
- Doubles
- Addition facts that make five
- Part-part-whole relationships (fact-family groups)
- Addition facts that make ten

First Grade:
- Part-part-whole relationships (fact-family groups): 0+5 = 5 and 5+0 = 5; 1+4 = 5 and 4+1 = 5; 2+3 = 5 and 3+2 = 5, and so on with other fact-family groups
- Anchors of 5 and 10 (five-frame and ten-frame)
- Counting by a given number (2s, 5s, 10s)
- Two more and two less than a number
- Addition and subtraction as inverse operations

Second Grade:
- Part-part-whole relationships in addition: 5 + 3 = 8; 3 + 5 = 8; 6 + 2 = 8; and 2 + 6 = 8; and so on
- "Think addition" for subtraction facts
- Addition and subtraction as inverse operations

Third Grade:
- Part-part-whole relationships (3 + 5 = 8; 2 + 6 = 8; 4 + 4 = 8; 8 - 5 = 3; 8 - 6 = 2; and so on) inboth addition and subtraction
- Regular practice with various patterns within multiplication facts (2s, 3s, 5s, 9s, 10s, and so on)
- Regular opportunities to develop a strong foundation with multiplication facts
- Strategy of "think multiplication" for division facts
- Multiplication and division as inverse operations

Step 4: Mastery of Math Facts

Using Patterns: A K-5 Summary *(Continued)*

Fourth Grade:

- Repeated practice with patterns within multiplication facts, division facts, and the number system (powers of 10)
- Strategy of "think multiplication" for division facts
- Multiplication and division as inverse operations
- Extend strategies to multidigit problems in Mental Math activities

Fifth Grade:

- Emphasize various patterns found within multiplication facts (i.e., 2s, 3s, 5s, 9s, 10s)
- Strategy of "think multiplication" with division facts
- Multiplication and division as inverse operations
- Determine a reasonable answer
- Apply math-facts strategies to multidigit problems provided during Mental Math activities

Middle School:

- The expectation is that students should enter middle school already having mastered their math facts.
- Middle school students should continue development of their number sense by receiving regular practice with the number-sense patterns and math-fact patterns developed in Grades K–5.

Suggestions for Daily Practice (Multiplication and Division)

- Orally practice all the twos, threes, fours, and so on with a family member, classmate, or teacher aide—first by groupings of like facts or in sequence, then at random, and finally with all the facts mixed together.
- Using flash cards, practice all the twos, threes, fours, and so on with a family member, classmate, or teacher aide— by groupings of like facts or in sequence, then at random, and then all together.
- Notice product *patterns* for multiplication:

    Look at product patterns for five (0, 5, 10, 15, 20, 25, 30, 35, 40, 45) where the ones digit alternates between zero and five.

    Look at product patterns of three (3, 6, 9 where 3 6 9) and the remaining products (12, 15, 18, 21, 24, 27) where the sum of the two digits equals three, six, or nine.

    Look at product patterns of nine (9, 18, 27, 36, 45, 54, 63, 72, 81, 90) where the sum of the two digits equals nine, the tens digits are sequenced in order from one to nine, and the ones digits are sequenced in reverse, from nine to zero.

- Count aloud the multiples of a given number.
- Learn the "Fact Families" in addition, subtraction, multiplication, and division.
- Write math facts each day in school and at home.
- Play math-facts games on the Internet and utilize computer software math-facts programs.
- Use practice worksheets.
- Read literature books that involve adding, subtracting, multiplying, and dividing in the story line.

Five Easy Steps Balanced Math Alignment Diagram

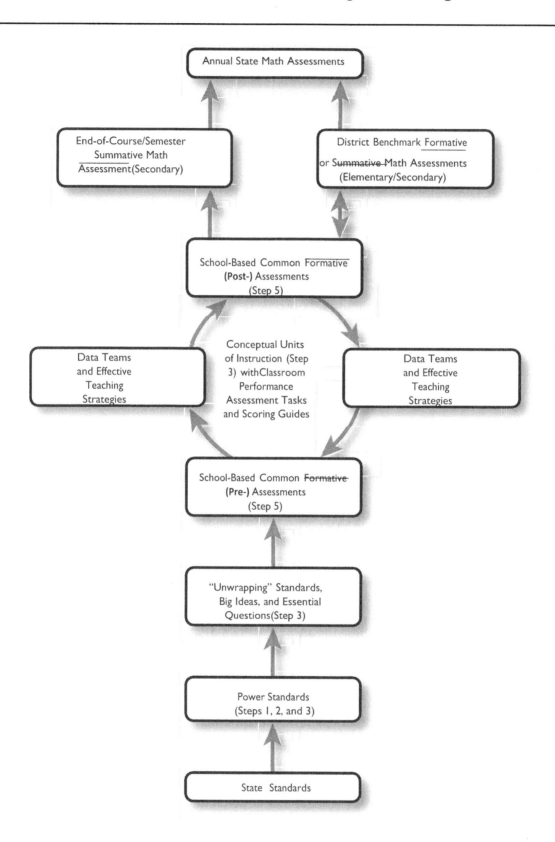

Annual State Math Assessments

End-of-Course/Semester Summative Math Assessment(Secondary)

District Benchmark Formative or Summative Math Assessments (Elementary/Secondary)

School-Based Common Formative (Post-) Assessments (Step 5)

Data Teams and Effective Teaching Strategies

Conceptual Units of Instruction (Step 3) withClassroom Performance Assessment Tasks and Scoring Guides

Data Teams and Effective Teaching Strategies

School-Based Common Formative (Pre-) Assessments (Step 5)

"Unwrapping" Standards, Big Ideas, and Essential Questions(Step 3)

Power Standards (Steps 1, 2, and 3)

State Standards

Adapted from *Common Formative Assessments: How to Connect Standards-Based Instruction and Assessment* (Ainsworth & Viegut, Corwin Press, 2006).

A Framework for Implementing

Five Easy Steps to a Balanced Math Program

What do math instruction and assessment *currently* look like in our school? (Sample responses)

Math Instruction	Math Assessment
• Varied approaches and styles • Mainly traditional approach • Textbook-driven • More lecture, less student involvement • Teacher-centered • Learning targets not always clear • Chapter-based vs. standards-based • Inch-deep, mile-wide coverage • Differentiation, but not enough to meet wide diversity of student needs • Monitoring/adjustment of instruction • Practice worksheets • Some peer tutoring • Some cooperative learning	• More summative than formative • Chapter and unit tests • District benchmark "dipstick" quarterly math assessments aligned to the state test • End-of-course assessments at secondary level • Certain schools are beginning to use common math assessments • Assessment not used to drive instruction

Step 1 Computational Skills (Math Review and Mental Math)

Current State	Action Steps	Desired State
•	•	• All grades using MR and MM daily
•	•	• Teacher-designed problems based on current needs of students
•	•	• Teachers emphasize reasonable answer and math strategies with students during processing of MR problems
•	•	• Math Review Quiz given weekly or biweekly
•	•	• Appropriate MR formats used at each grade level
•	•	• Math vocabulary incorporated into MR and MM
•	•	
•	•	
•	•	
•	•	

Step 2: Problem Solving

Current State	Action Steps	Desired State
•	•	• Core problem-solving strategies identified and used by all teachers
•	•	• Core problem-solving strategies taught to students
•	•	• Grade-level teams select or create multistep PSTs that match Conceptual Understanding Units
•	•	• Grade levels administer a PST at least twice a month
•	•	• Problem solving assessed with generic rubric applicable to all PSTs
•	•	• Students involved in self- and peer-assessment
•	•	• Students reflect on their progress (where they are doing well, where they need to improve) and develop goal/plan for improvement
•	•	• Ongoing support for teachers identified and provided as needed
•	•	
•	•	

Step 3: Conceptual Understanding

Current State	Action Steps	Desired State
•	•	• Conceptual teaching taking place at every grade level
•	•	• Grade-level mentor teachers assist colleagues with conceptual teaching as needed
•	•	• Core math standards (PS) identified and emphasized in conceptual units of instruction
•	•	• Math standards "unwrapped" to pinpoint key concepts and skills
•	•	• Big Ideas and Essential Questions used to focus instruction and assessment
•	•	• Math vocabulary identified and emphasized at each grade level
•	•	• Grade-level conceptual units, including aligned end-of-unit assessments, used to teach students "unwrapped" math PS concepts and skills
•	•	• School and/or district bank of grade-level math conceptual units established, for all teachers to use and contribute to
•	•	
•	•	

Five Easy Steps to a Balanced Math Program for Primary Grades

Step 4: Mastery of Math Facts

Current State	Action Steps	Desired State
•	•	• School plan in place that vertically maps all math facts in the four basic operations across grades K–5
•	•	• School plan reflects or clarifies the math facts listed in state standards
•	•	• Math-facts assessment schedule in place at each grade
•	•	• Parents and students understand school-wide plan and grade-specific assessment schedule
•	•	• Math facts taught through patterns, rather than memorization only
•	•	• Necessary resources are available for teaching and assessing students' mastery of grade-level math facts
•	•	
•	•	
•	•	
•	•	
•		

Step 5: Common Formative Assessment

Current State	Action Steps	Desired State
•	•	• Grade levels administer collaboratively designed, short-cycle math assessments *for* learning
•	•	• CFAs aligned to math PS and classroom end-of-unit assessments
•	•	• Assessments aligned to district quarterly math assessments
•	•	• CFAs include more than one type of format (selected response, short-constructed response, extended response)
•	•	• Grade levels collaboratively score math CFAs
•	•	• Grade levels analyze student data in grade-level or department Data Teams
•	•	• Assessment results used to differentiate instruction (interventions for students at risk and accelerations for proficient and advanced students)
•	•	
•	•	
•	•	

Five Easy Steps Prioritized Time Frame for Implementation

Time Frame—Year 1	What We Want to Have in Place
September (list school year)	•
October	•
November	•
December	•
January	•
February	•
March	•
April	•
May	•
June	•
Summer	•

Five Easy Steps Prioritized Time Frame for Implementation

Time Frame—Year 2	What We Want to Have in Place
August	•
September (list school year)	•
October	•
November	•
December	•
January	•
February	•
March	•
April	•
May	•
Summer	•

Five Easy Steps Prioritized Time Frame for Implementation

Time Frame—Year 3	What We Want to Have in Place
August	•
September (list school year)	•
October	•
November	•
December	•
January	•
February	•
March	•
April	•
May	•
Summer	•

What do math instruction and assessment currently look like in our school? (Add bullets as needed.)

Math Instruction	Math Assessment
•	•
•	•
•	•
•	•
•	•
•	•
•	•
•	•
•	•
•	•
•	•
•	•

Five Easy Steps to a Balanced Math Program for Primary Grades

Step 1: Computational Skills (Math Review and Mental Math)

Current State	Action Steps	Desired State
•	•	•
•	•	•
•	•	•
•	•	•
•	•	•
•	•	•
•	•	•
•	•	•
•	•	•
•	•	•
•	•	•

Step 2: Problem Solving

Current State	Action Steps	Desired State
•	•	•
•	•	•
•	•	•
•	•	•
•	•	•
•	•	•
•	•	•
•	•	•
•	•	•
•	•	•
•	•	•

Five Easy Steps to a Balanced Math Program for Primary Grades

Step 3: Conceptual Understanding

Current State	Action Steps	Desired State
•	•	•
•	•	•
•	•	•
•	•	•
•	•	•
•	•	•
•	•	•
•	•	•
•	•	•
•	•	•
•	•	•
•	•	•

Step 4: Mastery of Math Facts

Current State	Action Steps	Desired State
•	•	•
•	•	•
•	•	•
•	•	•
•	•	•
•	•	•
•	•	•
•	•	•
•	•	•
•	•	•
•	•	•

Step 5: Common Formative Assessment

Current State	Action Steps	Desired State
•	•	•
•	•	•
•	•	•
•	•	•
•	•	•
•	•	•
•	•	•
•	•	•
•	•	•
•	•	•
•	•	•

Five Easy Steps Prioritized Time Frame for Implementation

Time Frame—Year 1	What We Want to Have in Place
August	•
September (list school year)	•
October	•
November	•
December	•
January	•
February	•
March	•
April	•
May	•
Summer	•

Five Easy Steps Prioritized Time Frame for Implementation

Time Frame—Year 2	What We Want to Have in Place
August	•
September (list school year)	•
October	•
November	•
December	•
January	•
February	•
March	•
April	•
May	•
Summer	•

Five Easy Steps Prioritized Time Frame for Implementation

Time Frame—Year 3	What We Want to Have in Place
August	•
September (list school year)	•
October	•
November	•
December	•
January	•
February	•
March	•
April	•
May	•
Summer	•

References and Other Resources

References

Ainsworth, L. (2003a). *Power standards: Identifying the standards that matter the most.* Englewood, CO: Lead Learn Press.

Ainsworth, L. (2003b). *"Unwrapping" the standards: A simple process to make standards manageable.* Englewood, CO: Lead Learn Press.

Ainsworth, L., & Christinson, J. (2000). *Five easy steps to a balanced math program: A practical guide for K-8 classroom teachers.* Englewood, CO: Lead Learn Press.

Ainsworth, L., & Christinson, J. (1998). *Student generated rubrics: An assessment model to help all students succeed.*

New York: DaleSeymour Publications.

Ainsworth, L., & Viegut, D. (2006). *Common formative assessments: How to connect standards-based instruction and assessment.* Thousand Oaks, CA: Corwin Press.

Burns, M. (2004, October). Writing in math. *Education Leadership, 62*(2), 30–33.

Burns, M. (1999). Timed tests. In *Teaching children mathematics* (pp. 408–409). Sausalito, CA: NCTM.

Cawelti, G. (Ed.). (1999). *Handbook of research on improving student achievement* (2d ed.). Arlington, VA: Educational Research Service.

Hiebert, J. (1997). *Making sense: Teaching and learning mathematics with understanding.* Portsmouth, NH: Heinemann Press.

Hiebert, J. (2003, April 2). Taped lessons offer insights into teaching. *Education Week, (22)*29, 1, 24.

Ma, L. (1999). *Knowing and teaching elementary mathematics.* Mahwah, NJ: Lawrence Erlbaum Associates.

Marzano, R. J. (2004). *Building background knowledge for academic achievement.* Alexandria, VA: ASCD.

Marzano, R. J. (2003). *What works in schools: Translating research into action.* Alexandria, VA: ASCD.

Marzano, R. J. (2001, September 15). How and why standards can improve student achievement: A conversation with Robert J. Marzano. *Educational Leadership, 59*(1), 14–15.

National Council of Teachers of Mathematics. (2000). *Principles and standards for school mathematics.* Reston, VA: National Council of Teachers of Mathematics.

National Education Association. (2003). *Balanced assessment: The key to accountability and improved student learning.* Washington, DC: National Education Association.

Ruthven, R. (2005). *Nonfiction writing prompts for math (lower elementary).* [Write to Know series.] Englewood, CO: Lead Learn Press.

Seeley, C. L. (2005, December). Do the math in your head! *NCTM News Bulletin, (42)*5, 3.

Stiggins, R. J., Arter, J. A., Chappuis, J., & Chappuis, S. (2004). *Classroom assessment for student learning: Doing it right—using it well.* Portland, OR: Assessment Training Institute.

Van De Walle, J. (2004). *Elementary and middle school mathematics.* Boston: Pearson.

Wiggins, G., & McTighe, J. (1998). *Understanding by design.* Alexandria, VA: ASCD.

Webliography of Online Math

A Math
> http://www.aplusmath.com/

AAA Math
> http://www.aaamath.com/

AIMS Puzzles
> http://www.aimsedu.org/Puzzle/PuzzleList.html

Algebra Help
> http://www.algebrahelp.com/index.jsp

Algebra links (Purplemath)
> http://www.purplemath.com/internet.htm

Algebra S.O.S. Math
> http://www.sosmath.com/algebra/algebra.html

Algebra Tutor
> http://www.algebratutor.org

All Math
> http://www.allmath.com/

Applets for Teachers
> http://www.geocities.com/appletsforteachers/

ArithmAttack
> http://www.dep.anl.gov/aattack.htm

Ask Dr. Math
> http://mathforum.org/dr.math/

Aunty Math/Math Challenges
> http://www.dupagechildrensmuseum.org/aunty/index.html

Calculators Online
> http://www.math.com/students/tools.html

Cats in Line Activity Page
> http://www.janbrett.com/piggybacks/ordinal.htm

Cool Math 4 Kids

http://www.coolmath4kids.com/

Count On Math Games

http://www.counton.org/

Count Us In Game

http://www.abc.net.au/countusin/default.htm

Create a Graph

http://nces.ed.gov/nceskids/Graphing/

Disaster Math Word Problems

http://www.fema.gov/kids/dizmath.htm

Elementary Mathematics

http://www.bcps.org/offices/lis/curric/elem/mathematics.html

Enchanted Mind Tangram Puzzle

http://enchantedmind.com/puzzles/tangram/tangram.html

Fractals: Art or Math?

http://www.dcet.k12.de.us/teach/quest/shari.htm

Franklin Institute Mathematics Hotlist

http://www.fi.edu/tfi/hotlists/math.html

Fresh Baked Fractions

http://www.funbrain.com/fract/index.html

Funbrain Math Games

http://www.funbrain.com/

Gamequarium

http://www.gamequarium.com/math.htm

Geometry Dictionary

http://www.math.okstate.edu/~rpsc/dict/Dictionary.html

Geometry Online

http://math.rice.edu/~lanius/Geom/

History of Mathematics Archive

http://www-groups.dcs.st-and.ac.uk:80/~history/

iFigure: Online Calculators
    http://www.ifigure.com/

iMath Investigations
    http://illuminations.nctm.org/imath/

Improving Measurement & Geometry in Elementary Schools (IMAGES)
    http://www.dallassd.com/geometry/index.html

Interactive Mathematics
    http://www.cut-the-knot.org/content.shtml

Interactive Mathematics (Flash)
    http://teacherlink.org/content/math/interactive/flash/top.html

Interactive Word Problems
    http://www.geocities.com/Heartland/Ranch/2200/assess.htm

Kid's Clubhouse
    http://www.eduplace.com/kids/

Kids Domain Math Games
    http://www.kidsdomain.com/games/math2.html

King's Math Activities
    http://www.k111.k12.il.us/king/math.htm

Lemonade Stand
    http://www.lemonadegame.com/

Lite Brite (patterns)
    http://www.sfpg.com/animation/liteBrite.html

Magnetic Numbers
    http://home.freeuk.net/elloughton13/scramble1.htm

Math Cats
    http://www.mathcats.com/contents.html

Math Fact Cafe
    http://mathfactcafe.com/home/

Math Goodies
    http://www.mathgoodies.com/

Math in Daily Life
   http://www.learner.org/exhibits/dailymath/

Math Printables
   http://www.lr.k12.nj.us/ETTC/archives/drill.shtml

Math Stories (membership fee)
   http://www.mathstories.com

MathDrill
   http://www.mathdrill.com/index.php3

MathForum
   http://mathforum.org/

MATHGuide's Interactive Mathematics Lessons
   http://mathguide.com/lessons/

Mathnstuff.com
   http://www.mathnstuff.com

MathSURF Problem Solving
   http://www.mathsurf.com/teacher/index.html

Measure It!
   http://www.funbrain.com/measure/

Measure Your Weight on Other Worlds
   http://www.exploratorium.edu/ronh/weight/index.html

Measurement Games
   http://gamequarium.com/measurement.html

Measurement: Animal Weigh-In
   http://www.bbc.co.uk/education/mathsfile/shockwave/

MegaMathematics
   http://www.c3.lanl.gov/mega-math/

Megamaths
   http://www.bbc.co.uk/education/megamaths/tables.html

Moneyopolis
   http://www.moneyopolis.com/new/home.asp

Multiflyer

http://www.gdbdp.com/multiflyer/

Multiplication Rock

http://www.geocities.com/Athens/Academy/7303/M_Rock.html

National Library of Virtual Manipulatives

http://matti.usu.edu/nlvm/nav/grade_g_2.html

National Math Trail

http://www.nationalmathtrail.org/front2.html

Online Math Tools

http://www.gamequarium.com/onlinemathtools.html

Pattern Blocks

http://www.arcytech.org/java/patterns/patterns_j.shtml

PBS Mathline

http://www.pbs.org/teachersource/math.htm?default

Peg Strategy Game

http://scv.bu.edu/htbin/pegs

Ribbit's Math Ventures

http://www.mohonasen.org/staffdev/mathven/Ribbit/rdefault.htm

Room 108 Math Activities

http://www.netrover.com/~kingskid/108.html

Sea Shell Rounding Activity Page

http://www.janbrett.com/piggybacks/rounding.htm

Snapdragon (Telling the Time)

http://www.bbc.co.uk/wales/snapdragon/yesflash/intro.htm

Solving Math Word Problems

http://studygs.net/mathproblems.htm

Stanley Park Chase (multiplication)

http://www.bonus.com/bonus/card/stanley.bottom.html

Study Works: Puzzle of the Week (see also Puzzle Archives)

http://www.studyworksonline.com/cda/justforfun/main/0,,NAV3-39,00.html

Take A Challenge
   http://www.figurethis.org/index40.htm

Tangram Puzzle
   http://www.fwend.com/tangram.htm

The Spanky Fractal Database
   http://spanky.triumf.ca/

Visual Fractions
   http://www.visualfractions.com

Word Problems for Kids
   http://www.stfx.ca/special/mathproblems/welcome.html

Zone 101
   http://www.zone101.com/Pages/zkids.htm

Suggested Reading

Chappuis, S., Stiggins, R. J., Arter, J., & Chappuis, J. (2004). *Assessment for learning: An action guide for school leaders.* Portland, OR: Assessment Training Institute.

Le Patner, M., Matuk, F. N., & Ruthven, R. (2005). *Nonfiction writing prompts for math, science, and social studies for kindergarten* (Write to Know Series). Englewood, CO: Lead Learn Press.

Guskey, T. R., & Bailey, J. M. (2001). *Developing grading and reporting systems for student learning.* Thousand Oaks, CA: Corwin Press.

Marzano, R. J. (2000). *Transforming classroom grading.* Alexandria, VA: ASCD.

O'Connor, K. (2002). *How to grade for learning: Linking grades to standards* (2d ed.). Glenview, IL: Pearson Education.

Ruthven, R. (2005). *Nonfiction writing prompts for math for lower elementary* (Write to Know series). Englewood, CO: Lead Learn Press.

Index

A

acceleration, 186, 193, 203, 229
  based on assessment results, 14,69, 71
  bonus problems as, 22–23
  maintaining challenges, 6, 19–20
  need for, 21
accountability, xxvii
  assessment for, 89–90, 100
  for mastery of math facts, 89parents and, 20, 159
  program for, xxix, 85, 88
accountability quiz. *See* Math Review Quiz
achievement
  below grade level, 186
  improving, 176
  on tests, xxvi
activities, 70, 88
  deleting, 112
  formative, 72
  learning, xxvi, 56
  problem-solving, xxix. *See also* problem solving
  reporting, 36–37
  supplementing
  district program,xxvi
  addition, 11, 25, 129, 143
  facts that make five, 125, 139, 151
  facts that make ten, 125, 139, 151
  games using, 91
alignment diagram, 194–95, 208, 223
analytic rubrics, 50–51, 174
anchors of 5 and 10, 25, 139, 151
assessments. *See also* tests
  for accountability, 89–90, 100
  aligning to math focus, xxvi
  aligning with Conceptual Understanding Units, 108, 192
  aligning with instruction, xxix, 106
  aligning with standards, 109
  alternate methods, 97
  benchmark, 109–10, 224
  commercial, 90
  common formative. *See* common formative assessments
  diagnostic information from,32, 100, 163
  for differentiation of instruction, 69, 99, 188–89, 193, 203, 229
  district, 40, 109–11
  effective, xxiii
  end-of-unit. *See* end-of-unit assessments

assessments *(continued)*
external, 100
formative, 14–15, 72–73, 99
formats, xxiii, 90, 188, 193, 203, 229
to inform instruction, 3, 14–15, 21, 99, 100–101, 186
informal, 7, 15–16, 63, 69, 72–73, 106
interconnection of, 109–11, 113
internal, 100
item types, 126, 135, 140, 152
for learning, 72–73. *See also* common formative assessments
of learning, 100
multiple-measure, 113
parental review of, 90
by peers. *See* peer assessments
performance-based, 68, 69, 126, 140, 152
post-assessment. *See* post-assessment
practice with, 94–95pre-assessment. *See* pre-assessment
of problem solving, 47–55,192,200, 226
resources, 69
rubrics and. *See* rubrics
schedules, 89, 92, 188, 193, 202,228
of school's current reality, 196,198, 224, 233
scoring guides. *See* scoring guides self-assessment. *See* self-assessment
re standards, xxiv, 188
state, xxix, 40, 100, 104, 109–11, 176

students' use of, 100–101
summative, 100, 110
by teacher, 63, 73
teacher-created, 90
teaching students to do, 47, 73
timed, 93–96, 180, 181
traditional, 68, 69
types of, 68
of understanding, 15, 63, 119, 130, 144, 188
written, 8
assistance
dialogue for, 47
individual, 8, 23, 47
from parents, 20–21, 89
from peers, 5, 8, 19–20, 22, 164
during school day, 21, 23
small-group, 8, 22, 35
by student "experts," 12–13
from teacher, 8

B

balanced math program, xxiii, xxvii–xxviii
designing, xxviii–xxx
executive summary of, 185–89
preparation for implementation, 183
time frame for implementation, 186
Big Ideas
for Conceptual Understanding Unit topic, 76
developing, 79
identifying, 62, 66, 108, 192
as instructional guides, 201, 227
bonus problems
for advanced learning, 20
Math Review, 6, 16, 22–23, 164
processing, 129, 142

Burns, Marilyn, 5, 31–32, 85–86, 93

C

calculation errors, 51
Christinson, Jan, 82
clusters, 79
vocabulary, 82, 83collaboration
on common formative assessments, 99, 106–9, 188, 193
on Conceptual Understanding Units, 64, 70, 106–7, 175
in curriculum design, 179 grade-level teams, 51, 103, 108, 126, 140, 152
during Math Review, 8
opportunities for, 113 for
rubric design, 48
scoring assessments, 99, 203, 229
timeline for math-fact mastery, 87–88
common formative assessments, xxiv, xxix–xxx, 99–100. *See also* Step 5: Common Formative Assessment
administration schedule, 106, 108–9
aligning with Conceptual Understanding Units, 108
aligning with other assessments, 108, 189, 193, 203, 229
benefits of, 112–13
collaboration on, 99, 106–9, 188, 193
design of, 126, 140, 152
end-of-unit assessment similarity to, 106, 126,

Index

item types, 107
  for learning, 14, 18, 69, 100, 188, 193, 203, 229
  Power Standards and, 103, 126, 140, 153, 188, 193, 203, 229
  as pre- and post-assessments, 107–9
  pre-/post-assessment design, 188
  times administered, 188, 193
communication. *See also* Problem-Solving TaskWrite-Up Guide
  of mathematical thinking, 31, 32–33, 45
  of processes, 35, 37, 47, 171
  of understanding, xxiii, xxv, 52
  computational skills, xxiii, xxvi–xxvii, 72. *See also* Step 1: Computational Skills (Math Review and Mental Math)
  explanation of thinking, 32–33
  meaning-based, 3
  mental computation. *See* Mental Math
  practicing/reviewing, xxvii, 4, 5
concepts
  applying, 32, 33–34
  essential, 62, 66, 78–79, 101, 103
  identifying, 13
  review of, 4, 5
conceptual understanding, xxiii, xxiv–xxvii, 107. *See also* Step 3: Conceptual Understanding
  definitions of, 59–60
  developing, 14, 61
  need for, 176–77
  retaining, 3, 4

Conceptual Understanding Units, xxiv, xxix, 61, 201, 227
  aligning with assessments, 108, 192
  aligning with Power Standards, 105, 187, 201, 227
  aligning with rubrics/scoring guides, 192
  bank of, 187, 192, 201, 227
  collaboration on, 64, 70, 106–7, 175
  collaborative use of, 109
  components of, 76
  design template, 215–20
  designing and using, 62–63, 64–75, 175, 183
  duration of, 177
  focus of, xxix, 62, 64–65, 78
  informal assessment during, 106
  in instructional schedule, 160–61
  lesson planning and, 63, 70–71, 76
  number used per year, 175
  pacing schedules/charts and, 178
  problem solving and, 32
  Problem-Solving Tasks and, 33, 35, 172
  reader's assignment, 84
  relation of problems to, 4, 187, 191
  rubrics for, 63, 69–70
  sample, 76–77
  sample (grade 1), 135–38
  sample (grade 2), 148–51
  sample (kindergarten), 122–24
  self-reflection by teacher, 75
confidence, 9, 32, 45, 92
consistency, 113

cooperative groups, 35, 36–37, 133
counting, 25, 85
curriculum design, collaborative, 179

D

data analysis, 99, 108, 203, 229
  state assessment data, 100
Data Sheets, 36–37
  class, 120, 132
  directions for, 37
  group, 133
  independent completion of, 39
  individual, 122
  sample, 44
  transferring work from, 39 Data Teams, 108–9, 110, 193, 203, 229
differentiation of instruction, xxiv, xxx
  assessments for, 69, 99, 188–89, 193, 203, 229
  common formative assessment for, xxiv, 103
  mastery of math facts, 96–97
Math Review, 22–23, 164 Math Review Quiz for, 14–16
  problem-solving skills, 46–47
district math programs, xxv–xxvi
doubles, 25, 87, 91, 125, 139, 151
drawings. *See* graphic representation

E

early finishers, 6, 23
encouragement, 8
end-of-unit assessments, 63, 106, 152, 187, 203, 229. *See also* post-assessment

end-of-unit assessments
(continued)
  aligning with common
    formative assessments,
    108
  aligning with instruction, xxix
  common formative assessment
    similarity to, 106, 126, 140
  performance-based, 107
  sample (grade 1), 136, 137–38
  sample (grade 2), 150–51
  sample (kindergarten), 123
English-language learners, 18, 23
enrichment. *See* acceleration
equity, 177
error analysis, 165, 166
  in Math Review processing, 9
  by teacher, 23
  teaching how to do,
    10
  Essential Questions,
    xxx
    for Conceptual
      UnderstandingUnit topic,
      76
    developing, 79
    identifying, 62, 67–68, 108,
      192
    as instructional filter, 67, 70
    as instructional guide, 201,
      227Math Review Quiz, 14
  Mental Math, 24
  purposes of, 67
  responding to, 68–69
  sharing with students, 63, 71
  Step 1: Computational Skills
    (Math Review and
    MentalMath), 3
  Step 2: Problem Solving, 31
  Step 3: Conceptual
    Understanding, 59
  Step 4: Mastery of Math
    Facts,85
  Step 5: Common Formative
    Assessment, 99
estimation, 4, 66, 67

evaluation. *See* assessment
explanation of thinking, 32–33,
    170, 171

F

fact families, 25, 87, 139, 151
fact retrieval, strategies for,
    86–87, 97, 180, 181
feedback
  from assessments, xxx, 99
  Math Review Quiz as, 15
  professional, 179
  to students, 163, 173
  timely, 3, 17, 113
  via rubric, 53
first grade. *See* grade 1
Five Easy Steps program
  adapting, xxxi
  alignment diagram, 194–95,
    208, 223
  implementation framework,
    196–206, 224–41
  implementing, xxiii–xxiv, xxx,
    112, 185–206
  Step 1. *See* Step 1:
    Computational Skills (Math
    Review and Mental Math)
  Step 2. *See* Step 2: Problem
    Solving
  Step 3. *See* Step 3: Conceptual
    Understanding
  Step 4. *See* Step 4: Mastery of
    Math Facts
  Step 5. *See* Step 5: Common
    Formative Assessment
  time frame/timeline for
    implementation, 193, 197,
    204–6, 230–32, 239–41
  workshop, 187
five-frame, 25, 91, 129, 139, 151
flex groups, 8, 20, 22

folders
  for math-fact materials, 92 for
    student work product, 63,
    74–75
formative assessments, 14–15,
    72–73, 99. *See also* common
    formative assessments
forms. *See* reproducibles
frequently asked questions, xxxi,
    162–82

G

games, math-fact, 91
gap analysis, 104–5
geometry, 130
grade 1, 127–40
  Conceptual UnderstandingUnit,
    135–38
  mastery of math facts, 88, 139
  Math Review in, 7–8, 127–31
  Math Review Quiz in, 15–16,
    130–31
  Mental Math, 131
  problem solving, 132–34
  reflection methods, 18 rubric
    use, 55
grade 2, 141–53
  Conceptual UnderstandingUnit,
    148–51
  mastery of math facts, 88,151–
    52
  Math Review in, 8, 141–45Math
    Review Quiz in, 144 math
    schedule (sample),
    158–61
  Mental Math, 145
  problem solving, 146–47
  reflection methods, 18 rubric
    use, 55
grade 3, 88
grade 4, 88

Five Easy Steps to a Balanced Math Program for Primary Grades

grade 5, 88
grading. *See also* assessments;
     rubrics; scoring guides
     folders, 75
     nonmathematical criteria,
     173,
        174
     rubrics and, 173, 174
graphic representation, 47,
     187for demonstrating
        understanding, 7
     use with Problem-Solving
        Tasks, 35, 132
guidance. *See* assistance

H

holistic rubrics, 50–51, 174
homework, 20, 177

I

improvement, 9
     assessment for, 14
     instructional practice
        connection to, 112
     planning for, 15, 18
     student reflection on, 72–73,
        166, 192, 200, 226
indicators, 76, 84
instruction
     ability for, 179
     aligning with assessments,
        xxix, 106
     aligning with math focus,
        xxvi
     aligning with standards, 61
     assessment to inform, 3,
        14–15, 21, 99, 100–101,
        186
     balanced. *See* balanced math
        program
     conceptual, 80, 176–77, 192,
        201, 227

conceptual-unit approach, 60,
     72. *See also* Conceptual
        Understanding Units
     consistency in, 191
     differentiation of. *See*
        differentiation of instruction
     drill-and-kill, xxvii, 86, 180,
        188, 193
     effectiveness of, xxviii, 21, 99
     framework for, xxvi, xxviii
     international, 179
     mapping across grades, xxiv,
        xxix, 188, 192
     on math facts, 93–94
     meaning-based, 61
     modifying, xxx, 3, 72–73, 165
     modifying per assessment
        results, 14–15, 21, 106
     narrowing, 101
     pacing, xxvi
     from peers, 5. *See also* peers
     planning, 64, 71
     procedural, 80–81
     procedure-driven, xxv, 3, 4
     professional practice
        implementation, 112
     re-teaching, 6
     school's current reality, 198,
        224, 233
     teacher-directed, 9, 10
     textbooks as guides for,
        174–75
     time for, 101–2, 158
     whole-class, 35–36
instructional hours, 101–2
instructional level, 34, 46
instructional sequence, 159–60
Internet, 91, 173
interventions, 186, 193, 203, 229
     based on assessment results,
        14, 69, 72
     need for, 21

inverse operations, 61, 87, 139,
     152

J

journals, 82
judgment, professional, 178

K

kindergarten, 117–26, 120–22

     Conceptual Understanding
        Unit, 122–24
     mastery of math facts, 88, 125
     Math Review in, 7, 117–19
     Math Review Quiz, 15–16, 119
     Mental Math, 119–20
     problem solving, 120–22
     reflection methods, 18 rubric
        use, 55
knowledge package, 78, 179 knowledge
package process, 62,
        66, 78–81
     Koopsen, Scott, 19

L

leaders, school. *See* school leaders
leadership teams, 190–93
learning, 7
     assessment of. *See* assessments
     emphasis in, 86
     expectations, 76, 113
     meaning-based, 176
     reinforcing, 4
     responsibility for, 3, 74
     student reflection on, 3, 8, 74

     learning objectives, xxv
lesson planning
     backward planning, 106
     for Conceptual Understanding
        Units, 63, 70–71, 76

Lesson Study, 179
literature, 91

M

Ma, Liping, 78
manipulatives, 22, 47, 169
    use in grade 1, 128, 132
    use in kindergarten, 7,
        118
    use with Problem-Solving
        Tasks, 35, 41
Marzano, Robert, 81–82, 101–2
mastery of math facts, xxiv. *See
        also* Step 4: Mastery of
        MathFacts
    assessment schedule, 193,
        202,
        228
    counting on fingers, 181
    in daily instruction, 182
    differentiation of instruction,
        96–97
    elementary school
        responsibility for, 85, 188,
        202, 228
    grade 1, 88, 139
    grade 2, 88, 151–52
    kindergarten, 88, 125
    parents and, 88, 89, 94, 97,
        182
    patterns for. *See* patterns
    retrieval strategies, 180
    timed work and, 180–81
    timeline for, 85, 87–88, 89–
        90,97
    math facts
    grade-appropriate, 87–89
    identifying knowledge of, 96
    mastery of. *See* mastery of
        math facts
    memorization of, 85–86, 180
    practicing, 86, 90–92, 97, 125,
        139, 151
    state standards re, 202, 228

Math Forum, 34
math problems. *See* problems
math programs, district, xxv–xxvi
Math Review, xxiv, xxix. *See also*
        Step 1: Computational Skills
        (Math Review and Mental
        Math)
    bonus problems, 6, 16, 22–23,
        164
    conceptual unit relation, 72
    daily, 162
    as diagnostic process, 164–65,
        166
    differentiating, 22–23, 164
    difficulty level and
        progression, 5–6
    executive summary, 186–87
    formats, 191, 199, 225
    frequently asked questions,
        162–66
    grade 1, 7–8, 127–31
    grade 2, 8, 141–45
    independent, 10, 127
    key points in processing, 9–10,
        11
    kindergarten, 7, 117–19
    math-fact practice during, 90,
        92
    new concepts during, 5
    new material in, 164
    number of problems, 127, 163
    problem creation for, 164–65
    problem selection, 4, 5–6
    problem types, 15, 163, 164
    purposes of, 4, 15
    reproducibles, 209–11
    self-reflection during, 166
    teacher's role during, 8
    teaching sequence (grade 1),
        128
    teaching sequence
        (kindergarten), 118

    time for, 118, 129, 142, 163
Math Review processing, 9–14,
        18, 164
    methods, 10–14
    sequence (grade 1), 128–30
    sequence (grade 2), 142–44sequence
        (kindergarten),
        118–19
    student-directed, 10, 12
    time for, 9, 13–14
Math Review Quiz, 14–21, 186,
        191
    Essential Questions, 14
    format, 16
    grade 1, 15–16, 130–31
    grade 2, 144
    kindergarten, 15–16, 119
    need for, 163–64
    parental review of, 20
    proficiency, 16
    rationale for, 14–15
    sample, 17
    scoring, 17–18
    times used, 199, 225
    tutors, 16
Math Review Template, 6–7, 207,
        209–11
    grade 1, 127–28
    grade 2, 141–44
    kindergarten, 117
math vocabulary. *See* vocabulary
Math Word Wall, 13, 47
mathematical reasoning, 5, 51
    applying, 31, 33–34
    developing, xxiii, 118, 128
    explaining, 31
    in grade 2, 142
    modeling, 45
measurement, 11, 25
    grade 1 problems, 130
    grade 2 problems, 144
    kindergarten problems, 119

memorization, xxv, 85–86, 188, 193, 202, 228
  emphasis on, xxvi–xxvii of math facts, 85–86, 180
  methods, 94
  procedural learning, 176–77
Mental Math, xxiv, xxix. *See also*
    Step 1: Computational Skills(Math Review and Mental Math)
  benefits of, 28
  conceptual unit relation, 72
  Essential Questions, 24
  executive summary, 186–87
  frequently asked questions, 166–70
  grade 1, 131
   grade 2, 145
  grading, 167–68
  implementing, 25–27
  kindergarten, 119–20
  math-fact practice during, 90, 92, 97
  number-sense development and, 181
  participation in, 168–69
  problems for, 5, 27, 28, 166–67,168
  rationale for, 24
  regular practice of, 167
  repetition of problem, 26,169
  resources for, 28, 166–67
  student-created problems, 27
  teacher's ability, 170
  themes for, 25–26, 120, 131, 145, 167, 169
  time needed for, 26–27
  when to do, 25, 167
mentors and mentoring, 192,201, 227
metaphors, 83

Mid-continent Research for Education and Learning (McREL), 102
mistakes, 3, 9, 13
misunderstandings
  common, 3, 169
  insight into, 14, 32
  student awareness of, 3
  use of in Math Review processing, 18
modeling, 10
  exemplary work, 55, 73
  Problem-Solving Task work, 35, 36–37, 45
  proficient work, 55, 73
money units, 144

N

National Council of Teachers of Mathematics (NCTM), xxviii, 24, 31
National Education Association, 100
note taking, 10
notebooks, 82
number facts, 25
number sense, 3, 5
  daily practice with, 24
  development of, xxix, 14, 92, 97, 167, 180–81, 182
  development strategies, 118
  in grade 1, 128, 131
  in grade 2, 142, 145
  in kindergarten, 119, 125
  math-fact mastery and, 180
  progression through grade span, 7–8
  strategies, 9
number system, 180
  patterns in. *See* patterns
  understanding of, 9, 92

O

one more/one less, 87, 90, 118, 125, 139, 151
operations, 86, 92

P

pacing schedules/charts, 165, 178–79
parents
  accountability and, 20, 159
  assistance from, 20–21, 89
  informing of progress, 90, 95, 96
  math-fact mastery and, 88, 89, 94, 97, 182
  number-sense developmentand, 182
  review of student work, 20, 75
part-part-whole relationships, 25, 87, 139, 151, 152, 221
part-whole relationships, 11
"Pass the Pen," 12
patterns, 13, 119
  emphasizing, 86–87, 96
  in grade 1, 129
  in grade 2, 151–52
  knowledge of, 180
  mastery of math facts through, 86–87, 97, 180, 188, 193, 202, 228
  Mental Math themes and, 169
  number-sense, 125, 139, 151–52
  summary, 221–22
  understanding of, xxix
peer assessments, 63, 73, 192, 200, 226
peers
  assistance from, 5, 8, 19–20, 22, 164

peers *(continued)*
  guidance from, 5
  interaction with, 171
performance. *See also*
proficiency
  beginning, 52–53
  criteria, 48
  exemplary, 52
  levels, 50
  progressing, 52–53
  reflection on, 15, 18
performance assessment. *See*
  assessments
pictures. *See* graphic
  representation
place value, 11, 61, 81, 143
portfolios, 75
post-assessment, 63, 68–70, 73.
  See also common
  formative assessments
  aligning with pre-assessment,
    99, 108, 188
  common formative
    assessmentas, 107, 109
  sample, 76, 77
Power Standards, xxix–xxx,
  101–3
  aligning with Conceptual
    Understanding Units, 105,
    187, 201, 227
    assessment of,
      188
  common formative
    assessmentand, 103, 126,
    140, 153, 188,
    193, 203, 229
  gap analysis, 104–5
  identifying, 61, 103–5, 108,
    176, 192, 201, 227
  Mental Math themes and,
    169
  relation of math problems to,
    187
  "unwrapping," 108, 187, 192,
    201, 227

vertical alignment by grade,
  102–5
practice, 97
  assessments for, 94–95
  benefits of, 40
  of computational skills, xxviii,
    xxvii, 24
  for developing number sense,
    119, 131, 145
  effective, 181
  extra, 96
  feedback and, 3
  materials for, 90–91
  of math facts, 86, 90–92, 97,
    125, 139, 151
  Math Review as, 8
  parental assistance with, 20–21
  regular, 24, 167, 186
  skills, 165, 177
  in standards/strands, 4
  of strategies, 40
  understanding and, 6
pre-assessment, 63, 70, 71
  aligning with post-assessment,
    99, 108, 188
  common formative assessment
    as, 107
  to inform instruction, 106
  scoring, 63, 70, 71–72
  Step 4: Mastery of Math Facts,
    90
*Principles and Standards for
  School Mathematics* (NCTM),
  31
problem solving. *See also* Step 2:
  Problem Solving
  assessment of, 47–55, 192, 200,
    226
  in balanced math program,
    xxiv, xxvii
  independent, 35
  Math Review processing, 9–10

multiple approaches to problem,
  xxv, 4–5, 34, 43, 46,
  92, 133
  sequence, 45
  steps, 41–43, 214
  strategies, 40–41, 46, 191, 200,
    226
  structured activities for, 56
  success with, 172
  teacher's ability to do, 171–72
  teaching sequence, 120–22
  teaching sequences (grade 1),
    132–33
  teaching sequences (grade 2),146
  value of, 170–71
  word problems, 171–72 problems.
See also Problem-
  Solving Tasks
  bonus. *See* bonus problems
  enriching or extending, 34, 43,
    46
  matching to Conceptual
    Understanding Units, 4, 187,
    191
  Math Review. *See* Math Review
  Mental Math. *See* Mental Math
  multiple-step, 187, 191
  student needs and, 165–66,
    199, 225
  teacher's understanding of, 34,
    173, 179
  word. *See* word problems
problem-solving skills, 45
  math strategies, 186
  promoting, xxv, xxvi
Problem-Solving Tasks, 33, 183
  bank of, 173
  Conceptual UnderstandingUnits
    and, 33, 35, 172
  creating/selecting, 172–73,
    200, 226

criteria for good, 33–34
Data Sheets for, 36
difficulty level, 172
elements of, 51
independent completion of,
    133
initial, 47
in instructional schedule,
    160–61
instructional sequence for
    teaching, 35–40
reporting cooperative
    groupwork, 36–37
resources for
    finding/creating, 34
revising work on, 55
rubrics for. See rubrics
sample, 44
sample (grade 1), 134
sample (grade 2), 146–47
sample (kindergarten), 121
selecting, 33–34, 43, 46
teaching students to solve,
    35–40, 45
when to introduce, 158, 159
Problem-Solving Task Write-
Up, 37, 39, 132
Problem-Solving Task Write-Up
    Guide, 37–39, 187
following directions for,
    51frequency of use, 192
in rubric creation, 51–52
sample, 44
template, 57, 212
process, 32–33, 51
professional development,
    xxiv–xxv, 191, 192
proficiency, 48
    criteria for, 52, 113
    demonstrating, 16, 55
programs, commercial, 165–66
proof, 51, 171

Q

quality, 73
quantity, 125, 139, 151

R

reasonable answer, 4, 186
    emphasizing, 9, 92, 191, 199, 225
    Mental Math and, 170
reasoning ability, xxiii, 170
reasoning, mathematical. See
    mathematical reasoning
Reeves, Douglas B., 105, 178
reflection
    on improvement, 72–73, 166,
        192, 200, 226
    methods, 18
    oral, 18
    on learning, 3, 8, 74
    on performance, 15, 18
    questions for, 74
    self-reflection by teacher, 75
    student self-reflection, 18, 63,
        74, 166
regrouping, 78–81
remediation. See interventions
reproducibles, xxxi
    implementation framework,
        196–206, 224–41
    Math Review, 209–11
    problem solving, 213
    Problem-Solving Task Write-Up
        Guide, 212
    Problem-Solving Task Write-Up
        Guide templates, 187
    scoring guides, 213, 219
    Step 1: Computational Skills
        (Math Review and Mental
        Math), 207, 209–11, 234
    Step 2: Problem Solving, 207,
        212–14, 235

Step 3: Conceptual Under-
    standing, 207, 215–20, 236
Step 4: Mastery of Math Facts, 207,
    221–22, 237
Step 5: Common Formative
    Assessment, 208, 223, 238
re-teaching, 6
review. See Math Review
revision, 53, 55
Row or Group Expert, 12
Row or Group Representative, 12–
    13
rubrics
    aligning with Conceptual
        Understanding Units, 192
    analytic, 50–51, 174
    assessments with, 53–56
    benefits of, 56
    for Conceptual Understanding
        Units, 63, 69–70
    creating with students/ colleagues,
        48–49, 53, 55, 183
    criteria in, 48–53
    design of, 48, 50–53, 69–70
    formats for, 50–51
    generic, 174, 200, 226
    grading and, 173, 174
    holistic, 50–51, 174
    levels in, 50, 53
    over-rubricizing, 49
    problem-solving, xxix, 47–56,
        174, 187, 192
        purposes of, 173
    sample, 54
    task-specific, 135
    use for assessment, 53–55

S

schedule. See time managementschool
leaders
    guidelines for, xxxi, 185–206

school leaders *(continued)*
   leadership teams, 190–93
scoring
   collaborative, 99, 203, 229
   standardized tests, 181
   by teacher, 95
scoring guides, xxix. *See also*
      rubrics
   aligning with common
      formative assessments,
      108
   aligning with Conceptual
      Understanding Units, 192
   for post-assessment, 63, 69–
      70,73
   for pre-assessment, 63, 70,
      71–72
   reproducibles, 213, 219
   sample, 76, 77
   sample (grade 1), 137
   sample (grade 2), 150–51
   sample (kindergarten), 124
secondary grades, 158
Seeley, Cathy L., 24
selected-response items, 135
   self-assessment, 53, 56, 63,
         73
   by student, 187, 192, 200,
      226
self-concept, 85, 113–14
self-esteem, 93
sense-making, 47
similes, 83
skills. *See also* computational
      skills
   applying, xxiii, 32, 56, 170,
      187
   building, 162, 163
   essential, 101, 103
   practicing, 165, 177
   problem-solving.
   See problem-
   solving skills
   retaining, xxvii, 3,
   4, 24
   reviewing, 4

special education students, 18
special-needs students, 169
Speedy System, 12
spiral review, 165–66
standards
   alignment with assessments,
      109
   assessment regarding, xxiv,
      188
   in Conceptual Understanding
      Units, 76
   covering, 175–76
   essential, xxix, 61, 99, 176, 178.
      See also Power Standards
   essential topics in
   grade-level, 62, 65, 174–75,
      176
   for mastery of math facts,87–
      88, 202, 228
   number of, xxv, 101–2
   Power Standards. *See* Power
      Standards
   problems matched to, 4, 34
   problems representing, 5
   targeted, 126, 140, 152
   "unwrapping," 62, 65–66, 78
Step 1: Computational Skills
      (Math Review and Mental
      Math), xxix, 3–29. *See also*
      computational skills
   Essential Questions, 3
   executive summary, 186–87
   frequently asked questions,
      162–70
   grade 1, 127–31
   grade2,141–45
   implementation framework,
      199, 225, 234
   implementing, 29
   kindergarten, 117–20
   leadership team planning
      questions, 191

   Math Review component,
      4–23. *See also* Math Review
   Mental Math component,
      24–28. *See also* Mental Math
   rationale for, 3
   reader's assignment, 28–29
   reproducibles, 207, 209–11,
      234
Step 2: Problem Solving, xxix,31–
      57. *See also* problem solving
   assessment of, 47–55
   benefits of, 56
   differentiation of instruction,46–
      47
   Essential Questions, 31
   executive summary, 187
   frequently asked questions,
      170–74
   grade 1, 132–34
   grade 2, 146–47
   implementation framework,
      200, 226, 235
   implementing, 57
   kindergarten, 120–22
   leadership team planning
      questions, 191–92
   problem-solving process, 33
   problem-solving sequence, 45
   rationale for, 31–33
   reader's assignment, 57
   reproducibles, 207, 212–14,
      235
   rubrics in. *See* rubrics scoring
   guides. *See* scoring
      guides
   selecting Problem-Solving Task.
      See Problem-SolvingTasks
   steps for problem solving,41–43
   time needed to teach, 45

Five Easy Steps to a Balanced Math Program for Primary Grades

Step 3: Conceptual Understanding, xxix, 59–84. *See also* conceptual understanding
  Essential Questions, 59
  executive summary, 187
  frequently asked questions, 174–79
  grade 1, 135–38
  grade 2, 148–51
  implementation framework, 201, 227, 236
  kindergarten, 122–24
  leadership team planning questions, 192
 rationale for, 60
  reproducibles, 207, 215–20, 236
Step 4: Mastery of Math Facts, xxix, 85–98. *See also* mastery of math facts
  assessment administration, 92, 95-96
  assessment alternatives, 97
  assessment preparation, 94–96
  assessment timeline, 89–90, 98
  differentiation of instruction, 96–97
  Essential Questions, 85
  executive summary, 188
  frequently asked questions, 180–82
  grade 1, 139
  grade 2, 151–52
  grade-appropriate facts, 87–89, 98
  implementation framework, 202, 228, 237
  implementing, 86–92
  kindergarten, 125
  leadership team planning questions, 192–93

  pattern emphasis, 86–87, 96
  pre-assessment, 90
  rationale for, 85–86
  reader's assignment, 98
  reproducibles, 207, 221–22, 237
Step 5: Common Formative Assessment, xxix–xxx, 99–114. *See also* common formative assessments
  aligning all assessments, 109–11
  designing assessments, 106–9
  Essential Questions, 99
  executive summary, 188–89
  grade 1, 140
  grade 2, 152–53
  implementation, 107–9, 203, 229, 238
  kindergarten, 126
  leadership team planning questions, 193
  rationale for, 100–101
  reader's assignment, 114
  reproducibles, 208, 223, 238
  resources re, 162
strategies, 186
  analyzing, 31
  choices of, 41
  computational, 4
  to develop number sense, 118
  development of, 24, 170
  exploring, 168
  for fact retrieval, 86–87, 97, 180, 181
  for incorporating writing into math program, 32
  math, 186, 191, 199, 225
  for math-fact retrieval, 180
  number-sense, 9
  practicing, 40
  problem-solving, 40–41, 46, 191, 200, 226

  sharing, 19, 34
  students' development of own, 24
  teaching, 188
subtraction, 11, 25, 61, 143
  games using, 91
  with regrouping, 78–81 "think addition" strategy, 152
  success, 97, 172
    immediate, 46
  preparation for, 40, 113
  promoting, 45
support materials, commercial, 166

T

teachers isolation
  of, 64
  support needs, 200, 226
  understanding of math, 34, 173, 179
teaching. *See* instruction
teaching strategies, 188 teams. *See* collaboration;
  cooperative groups; Data Teams templates. *See* reproducibles
ten-frame, 25, 91, 139, 151
tests. *See also* assessments
  achievement on, xxvi, 176
  formats, 188
  learning to take, 170 predictive value re, xxx, 189 preparation for state, xxix, 176 range of, xxvii
  standardized, 181
  timed, 93–96, 180, 181
textbooks, xxvi, 173
  adequacy of, 67
  conceptual-unit approach and, 61, 174–75

Index

textbooks *(continued)*
  problem-solving resources in,
    34
  review in, 177
time constraints, 93–96
time, lack of, xxv
time management, xxxi, 157–61
  classroom minutes allotted to
    math, 157–58
  weekly schedule, 43
topics
  choosing, 6–7, 108
  essential, xxix
transition words, 37, 39, 42
tutors and tutees, 16, 19–20

U

understanding. *See also*
    misunderstandings
  assessment of, 15, 63, 119, 130,
    144, 188
  checking, 163
  communicating, xxiii, xxv, 52
  conceptual. *See* conceptual
    understanding
  demonstrating, xxiii, 7, 68, 113
  depth of, 72
  emphasizing, 175–76
  essential, 64, 79, 81, 175
  insight into, 107
  of mathematics, 173
  from meaning-based
    instruction, 61

of number relationships, 86
of number system, 9, 92
of operations, 86
of patterns, xxix
practice and, 6
procedural, 59, 107
teacher's, 34, 173, 179

V

Van De Walle, John, 59–60, 86, 87
verification, 45, 51, 171
vocabulary, 186, 191
  assessment results and,
    81–82
  English-language learners and,
    23, 46
  in Math Review processing, 13
  in Mental Math, 25, 27
  posting, 32, 47
  in rubrics, 48
  saying a number, 125, 139, 151
  in Step 1, 199, 225
  in Step 3, 201, 227
  teaching, 82–83
  transition words, 37, 39
  use of, 31, 42, 45, 51

W

whole-class instruction, 35–36
word problems, 45, 171–72. *See
    also* Problem-Solving Tasks;
    problems

bonus problems in Math
    Review, 6
strategies for solving, 40–41
worksheets, 91
writing. *See also* Problem-Solving
    Task Write-Up
  communicating understanding
    in, xxv
  description of process, 187
  explanation of thinking, 170
  formats for. *See* Problem-Solving
    Task Write-Up Guide
  including in math program,
    31–32
  math vocabulary in, 13
  as problem-solving step, 42
  self-reflection and, 18, 63, 74
  sharing, 32
  transition words, 37, 39, 42

Z

zero, 87

Made in the USA
Las Vegas, NV
14 December 2024